GW00888719

CONTENTS

Thanks are due to the many teachers and students who invited me into their classrooms, and in particular to Laura Seex who generously shared with me her considerable knowledge of infant readers.

J.W.

This pamphlet is the direct result of a joint venture between the Schools Council and the Equal Opportunities Commission. The Schools Council is charged with developing the school curriculum, the EOC with the promotion of sex equality; in 1979 they decided to pool their expertise in these areas and to collaborate on a series of pamphlets in a range of curricular areas.

The Schools Council has affirmed its commitment to equal educational opportunities for girls and boys. It has set up a Sex Differentiation in Schools Working Party and has funded a number of activities aimed at reducing sex bias in education. The issue of sex differentiation is increasingly recognized as important. Research continues to demonstrate the sexual inequalities built into our educational system and many teachers are now actively involved in developing ways of reducing the disadvantages experienced by both girls and boys.

In the past most educational attention has been directed towards secondary schooling. This is understandable: secondary education introduces the notion of curriculum choice and subject specialization. At secondary level selection tends to be overwhelmingly sex-stereotyped and the impoverished curriculum experienced by girls and boys has been indicted in numerous HMI documents.

Although secondary education constructs these curricular barriers it is now clear that their foundations have been laid at an early age. Sexually constrained attitudes can also set up obstacles to genuine equality of opportunity. Judith Whyte's excellent study describes the range of sex-stereotyped practices that can be experienced by girls and boys during their primary education. Such practices are insidious because they are unconscious and yet particularly persuasive in their long-term effects on girls' and boys' abilities, aspirations and achievements. The author, a Director of the GIST Project,*has assembled a range of research evidence and school-based practices with clarity and care, and presents a compelling argument on the extent and effects of sex stereotyping at an early age. Her recommendations on good practice are both sensible and workable and should be of practical use to teachers.

Most important of all however is the clear message that sexual equality is dependent on eliminating sex bias in the earliest years of education, for which the commitment and support of primary teachers is a prerequisite. Without this volition 'equality of opportunity' is likely to remain an illusion; Judith Whyte's pamphlet should help the phrase to become a reality.

LESLEY KANT
Schools Council

---

* Girls into Science and Technology Project, Manchester Polytechnic, 9A Didsbury Park, Manchester M20 OLH.

1. WHAT'S WRONG WITH THE WENDY HOUSE?

Reference your S/C/298ST/JW dated 27th April 1981 and headed
"Sex-Stereotyping Working Party".

My very experienced admission class teacher said at 3.15 p.m.
yesterday, "It has taken me all day today to hear each child read".
I feel that this sums up my feelings about the activity form we
have been asked to fill in. In this school with large classes, we
do not have time for frivolities. I have never advocated children
wasting time playing with toys and as all our teaching is directed
teaching perhaps that is why we have so few problems.

I strongly feel that if the Education Office wishes to waste time
on such things then please don't ask me to waste the time of well
trained experienced teachers. I have managed to draw up a
satisfactory curriculum for twenty-four years without any help
from working parties.

'Sex stereotyping' is an inharmonious, ugly and still unfamiliar phrase.
It can raise hackles, as in this letter from a hardworking headteacher
who had many more pressing problems to deal with than such a 'frivolous'
issue.

   It is the argument of this pamphlet that far from being a 'frivolous'
question, the adaptation of children to sex role expectations can have
profound and damaging educational consequences for both sexes. This is
the reason and indeed the only justification for asking primary school
teachers to focus seriously and consciously on the difference that it
makes being a schoolboy or a schoolgirl.

   Our schools and our teachers are firmly committed to equality of
educational opportunity for girls and for boys. Almost all primary
schools are coeducational, reflecting our conviction that girls and boys
should be offered the same experiences at school.

   The idea that primary schools somehow discriminate against girls
seems, on the face of it, unlikely. After all, girls do so much better
than boys at primary school. They learn to read and count sooner and
their general intellectual achievement is superior right up to the age
of 11. It is only after that that girls' academic performance seems to
drop off in comparison with boys'. Surely if schooling is to blame at
all, the problem lies in secondary school?

   Many writers see subject choice at 13+ as the crux of the matter.
Adolescent girls, especially in mixed schools, are concerned - even
obsessed - with asserting their femininity. That concern provides a
strong counter-motive to choosing subjects with a 'masculine' image.
Unfortunately, the 'masculine' subjects - physics, chemistry, mathematics,
and craft, design and technology (CDT) - are the most useful for getting

into further education or secure jobs. But it is not simply misguided choices which are the problem. Girls perform less well than boys in some of these subjects at secondary school. They also behave differently in the classroom. The boy's learning style is active, participatory, demanding, lending itself to a confident, independent approach to learning. The girl's is more passive, less participatory, making fewer demands on the teacher's time and attention and leading to an underestimation of her own ability and a lack of confidence, especially in science and mathematics.

It is unlikely that these crucial differences between the sexes suddenly make their appearance at the age of 13. Their roots are to be uncovered in different patterns of growth in the primary years and in particular in the way that school prepares children for adult life.

Of course, a great deal of children's learning of sex roles occurs outside school: within the family or under the influence of the media. Chapter 2 summarizes some of the evidence about ways in which children adapt to the 'appropriate' sex role behaviour which parents and society at large expect of them. But it is not just parents who teach children that boys are more important. The message comes through all the more powerfully in school, where children are collected together in mixed groups. If schools and teachers seem to lay great stress on the difference between the sexes, and on traditional sex roles, they give a special seal of official approval which is absent from the more informal atmosphere of home.

The evidence is that boys and girls do receive very different educational 'packages'. Chapter 3 gives an account of the differential pattern of educational achievement between the sexes. Boys leave school with the more prestigious (because more marketable) qualifications. Girls of similar ability to their male peers drop out of the education system at an earlier age, and have considerably poorer prospects there-after. The phenomenon is so familiar it has become unremarkable; it is regarded as entirely natural, and even inevitable.

A teacher's attitude to children is coloured by unstated assumptions about future adult roles. Consciously or unconsciously teachers expect boys and girls to be different because they know men and women are different. But which differences are real? What if expectations bear more resemblance to the known past than the possible future? The radical changes in social and family life already require a different sort of man as well as a different sort of woman:

> 'Girls playing football. It's modern, it's great!' (Gregory, hero of the film *Gregory's Girl*)

The 'modern' man and woman

Traditionally, the pattern of a woman's life was dominated by her role as wife and mother. In 1854 it was a role literally fatal to some women. As Figure 1(a) shows, the average woman at that time had six children and was dead soon after she reached 40. The typical employed woman was a young unmarried working girl. One of the most significant changes in the lives of women in this century has been towards a two-phase working life. The trend was already well established by 1954. Large numbers of women, with fewer children and increased life expectancy, returned to the labour market after completing their families (see Figure 1(b)). These trends

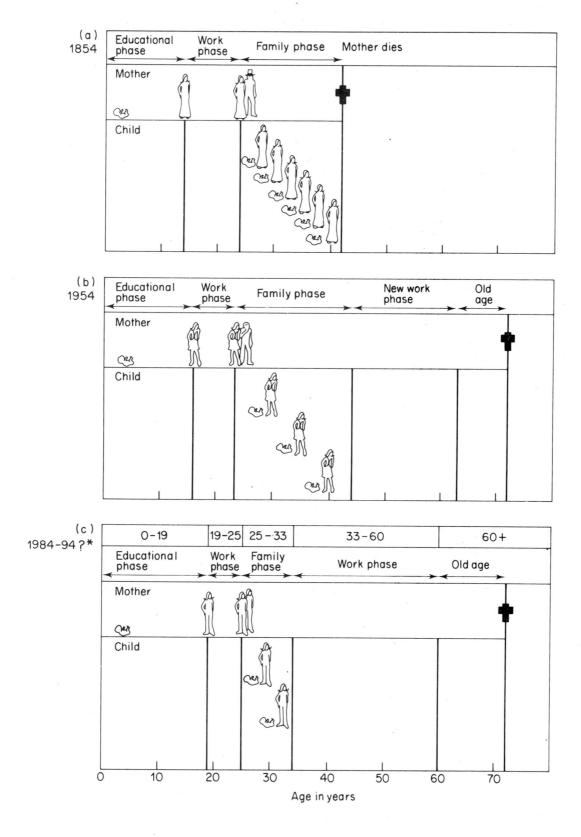

Figure 1 Development of women's two-phase working life.

Adapted from a diagram by Ann Oakley, in 'The myth of motherhood', *New Society*, 26 February 1970, p. 351. Source: A. Myrdal and V. Klein, *Women's Two Roles*, Routledge & Kegan Paul, 1956; Office of Population Censuses and Surveys, *General Household Survey*, 1976, Table 4.5; and Equal Opportunities Commission, *The Fact about Women is ...* (leaflet), 1982. *Based on current statistical trends, 1982.

have accelerated in the past thirty years. Figure 1(c) is based on current statistics and statistical projections.

Completed family size is now down to two; we are merely reproducing ourselves! With a longer educational phase, the *typical* working woman is more likely to be married, and to have completed her family.* The average break from employment is now as little as seven years. Girls at school today can expect to be in employment (or seeking it) for a period of up to twenty-five years after their children are born. Females make up 40 per cent of the workforce. Girls need to get from school a basis for economic survival. For this reason alone, it is time we abandoned the idea that boys' educational achievement is more important.

The work that women can do is not likely to remain the same as in the past. Most women are now employed in sectors of the economy where the majority of the workforce is female: office work, the distributive trades, the clothing industry and the service sector. Many of these 'feminine' occupations are contracting or disappearing altogether. New information technology is likely to reduce the number of office and secretarial jobs, and automation and recession will have a further impact on jobs in shops and the textile industry. The qualifications many girls obtain before they leave school are unlikely to be useful to them in the longer-term future.

The modern woman also makes considerably more demands on her partner than in the past. Men of all classes are becoming more home-centred, sharing housework and childcare with their wives. Mass unemployment may underline this trend. We cannot be sure that society in the future will require males to be full-time workers and breadwinners for the whole of their lives. Yet men are unprepared by their socialization for the future domestic role.

Generally speaking, males in our society have underdeveloped social and interpersonal skills. They have not learned to empathize with and listen to others. They have been socialized to see themselves as more important than females in social situations. Sensitivity and awareness of the needs of others are still seen as feminine rather than masculine qualities.

The 'hidden' curriculum

This booklet is for the primary teacher who is dissatisfied with the way that primary education prepares boys and girls for their future roles, but uncertain how far it is right and proper for schools to promote profound social change. It is *not* a booklet about discrimination. The vast majority of teachers are genuinely concerned to foster the development of all their children, both girls and boys.

However it is apparent that the experience of schooling itself exaggerates and reinforces the process of sex differentiation. Chapter 4 examines the evidence on the role of the school, and of the teacher in the classroom, in sex-typing.

---

* This idea is developed in Hakim (1979).

Despite boys' relatively poorer achievement in the primary years, teachers appear to have higher expectations of them. They are believed to be more creative and more 'truly' intelligent than girls. Boys' poorer behaviour in terms of junior school norms is accepted in a way that similar misbehaviour from girls would not be. Boys' greater difficulties in acquiring reading and language skills has led to enormous emphasis on these areas of the curriculum, but no parallel concern with girls' lack of visuo-spatial skills and their lesser confidence in pre-mathematical or scientific learning. Curriculum resources, teaching approaches and topic work are unduly geared towards boys' interests for a variety of reasons, some connected with boys' less compliant behaviour.

Within the peer group, girls and boys divide themselves competitively along sex lines and exclude one another from sex-typed activities, inside and outside the classroom. The organization of the primary school and classroom reinforces rather than challenges such patterns of sex antagonism. An unintended consequence is male dominance in the classroom, the playground, the sportsfield and in the experience of the primary school as a whole.

From the outset of schooling, girls are oriented towards the demands of the teacher rather than the task. While boys seek attention through aggression and rule-breaking, girls seek approval through conforming to pupil norms. Although girls' intellectual achievement is in general better than that of boys, they retreat from sex-competition, lack confidence and react more negatively to perceived failure. They comply with the male orientation of resources, tasks and norms and in so doing 'learn to lose'.

These processes are subtle, almost invisible. They are certainly an unintended consequence of 'education for equality'. The outcome is apparent in the secondary rather than the primary school. Yet we know that children have acquired a great deal of knowledge about sex role expectations before they ever get to secondary school. Much of that knowledge has been gained not only from the media and the family, but from other children, and even from the teacher, in infant and junior school.

The war of the sexes may be invisible to us because we take it so much for granted. But even the youngest children are in no doubt that there exist two mutually exclusive and frequently hostile groups. A current playground chant in the infant schools of Manchester is: 'Boys are fantastic, girls are elastic'. With the unerring instinct of the very young these children show us they know what lies behind the facade of sexual equality. The chant implies that boys are something special and primary, while girls are malleable, adaptable and secondary. It is possible that children's picture books and readers, often geared to boys' interests, and presenting girls and women in narrow traditional roles, have contributed to the child's view of what it is to be a girl or a boy. Chapter 5 discusses stereotyping in classroom materials, and what can be done to counter its effects.

Good practice

Primary schools may have been slow to catch up with social changes. But what can practically be done to ensure that both sexes develop as far as their individual qualities will allow, without the constraints of the

traditional sex role stereotypes? Chapter 5 contains practical
suggestions and strategies for good practice which can reasonably
be implemented, and in most cases have already been carried out in
one or more primary schools in the country.

> The break which must be made with the past is one which
> concerns everyone and especially those women to whom the
> education of children is confided. This rupture does not
> consist in shaping little girls into a masculine mould,
> but in ensuring that each individual is given the
> possibility of developing in whatever way suits them
> best, independently of the sex to which [they] belong.
> (Belotti, 1975, pp. 15-16)

The Wendy House

> *Domestic activities*: a wendy house or screened-off corner;
> dolls and dolls' clothes; furniture; tea-set; pram; beds
> and bed-clothes. Equipment for cooking (including recipes),
> cleaning, bathing dolls, washing clothes, shopping. (Anglo-
> American Primary Education Project, 1972, vol. 3, p. 101)

The Wendy House, or 'home corner' is an almost universal feature of
infant classrooms. Many educational functions are claimed for it. A
child can:

> rehearse adult roles or replicate some home experience in
> order to come to terms with it. He can re-explore a
> frightening or worrying experience or express the jealousy
> he feels for the new baby by being angry and aggressive
> with the inanimate baby, be a baby again or a mother or
> father or a wayward child. (Lancaster and Gaunt, 1976, p. 87)

Children should also be able to develop reading and writing skills by,
for example, making shopping lists, reading recipes, writing on the
telephone pad. Setting the table, dressing dolls in correctly-sized
clothes or redecorating the house can all provide concrete experiences
as a foundation for mathematical development.

These are the reasons usually given as to why there should be a Wendy
House in the classroom at all.

But the Wendy House is also an area in which girls predominate (see
Chapter 4, p. 32); it is the symbol and focus of home in the infant
classroom. If the school is a microcosm of society, the Wendy House may
be seen symbolically as representing the home, the 'feminine' sphere.
When the *boys* enter the Wendy House it is perhaps precisely in pursuit
of some of the educational objectives outlined above, but when *girls*
play there the focus of their activity is blurred. They may instead be
practising housework and childcare in imitative preparation for future
roles as wives and mothers.

The Wendy House can be of educational value; teachers believe that
the 'domestic activities' are used for educative rather than socializing
ends. But positive efforts need to be made to ensure this really happens.
If the bricks, trains and construction toys in other parts of the room
are rarely played with by girls, they will need specific encouragement
to move out towards this less familiar space, the 'masculine' sphere of
the world beyond the Wendy House.

The process cannot end there, however. Any changes in women's lives at once affect men too. By the same token, in the mixed primary school, intervention to redress the balance in favour of girls only would immediately affect boys, perhaps in counter-productive ways. The problem then is not only 'what shall we do to help the girls?', but 'how shall we prepare both sexes for living in a world where sexual demarcation is less rigid than in the past?'. For all our futures it will be just as important to have men who can be sensitive and caring, as to have women who can be independent, confident and competent. The Wendy House seems as good a place as any to start.

Overheard in the Wendy House:

You be the Daddy and get some ice cream and I'll be the Mummy, and stay at home and shout. (*Women and Education Newsletter*, no. 7, spring 1976)

References

Anglo-American Primary Education Project, 1972, *British Primary Schools Today*, vols. 1, 2 and 3, Macmillan.

Belotti, E.G., 1975, *Little Girls*, Writers and Readers Publishing Co-operative.

Hakim, C., 1979, *Occupational Segregation: A Comparative Study of the Degree and Pattern of the Differentiation Between Men's and Women's Work in Britain, the United States and Other Countries*, Research Paper no. 5, Department of Employment.

Lancaster, J. and Gaunt, J., 1976, *Developments in Early Childhood Education*, Open Books.

2. WHAT HAVE CHILDREN LEARNED BEFORE THEY COME TO SCHOOL?

Nursery and reception teachers are convinced they can see differences between girls' and boys' behaviour, attitudes and interests when they first come to school. When and how does this sex-typing occur? Is it inherent in the make-up of each sex, or the result of social learning?

Innate differences in behaviour

Adults often assume that differences between boys and girls are inborn or innate. That is why studies of very young infants aged less than one year are of great interest. It seems likely that any sex differences emerging so early in life must be natural rather than social in origin.

There have been literally hundreds of studies of the behaviour of boy and girl babies. A few studies of neonates showed up small differences, for instance in crying or feeding behaviour, or the need to be close to mother. It is difficult to say whether these studies take us much further towards finding 'innate' differences. In some cases, repeat experiments have failed to find the differences again. And it does not seem to be possible to show any connection between, for instance, babies who cry a lot and behaviour some months or years later. Other research shows that mothers treat boy and girl babies differently from the moment of birth. The problem is really that as early as one can find sex differences which may be biological in origin one can also find evidence of how society - in the shape of parents, siblings, media, nursery teacher or whatever - may have treated boys and girls differently, producing sex differences in behaviour.

Learned differences

Whatever the importance of biological or innate differences, there is no argument about whether children are in fact socialized into appropriate sex roles. It is clear that learning to behave in a 'masculine' or 'feminine' way is a crucial element in socialization. This chapter considers the ways in which children learn sex role stereotypes outside the school.

Direct comments

Adults socialize children and it is the job of parents to do so in the home. But adults in general feel it is their role to guide the children they meet in everyday situations.

Things adults say to children can teach them to associate masculinity or femininity with a number of other ideas. Children may learn to watch out for references to 'boy' or 'girl', 'pretty' or 'brave', because they

'The ideal couple'. Source: See Red Women's Workshop. This poster is out of print. For catalogue of 27 posters currently in print, write to 16a Iliffe Yard, off Crampton Street, London SE17.

know, without fully understanding why, that these terms are of specific interest to themselves.

That's a clever boy!

What a brave fellow!

Isn't she a pretty girl today!

Where's Daddy's girl?

On the whole, however, socialization processes are less direct than this.

Differential treatment

From the earliest age, girls are handled and cuddled more than boys, and treated more gently; they tend to be fed more often and picked up more quickly when they cry. Parents do treat their children differentially according to sex. It seems that fathers are more anxious that their children should conform to sex stereotypes, but mothers too respond differently to sons and daughters from the moment of birth. (This kind of differential treatment is largely unconscious, and has only emerged from painstaking and detailed research.) It is as if parents, without being aware of it, had determined to be harder on the son from the start, feeling 'he will have to stand up for himself'.

As adults, we are not always aware of how quick children are to pick up clues about what we find pleasing. Boys think adults don't like them as much; girls see themselves as more accepted and they value themselves more than boys do. This corresponds to the finding that boys believe teachers dislike boys and prefer girls (Hartley, 1978). Perhaps because their treatment has been altogether gentler and more sympathetic from the outset, girls are more eager to please grown-ups, and our differential treatment continues and confirms this tendency.

As far as girls are concerned, the role of the father can be more important than has been recognized in the past. Fathers spend less time with their children, yet their influence is quite considerable. Babies see fathers as a source of security in an unfamiliar setting as early as they see mothers.

Role modelling

It is easy to forget that it takes children some years to become assured of their own sex identity. Until then, they can suffer considerable uncertainty about whether they will always be the sex they are now. Young children may believe that sex is determined by behaviour, clothing, hair-styles or toys. Unless we tell them, they do not immediately realize that anatomical differences are the key factor. The understanding that sex identity is permanent can be arrived at at any time between the ages of 3 and 4 to 7 or even 8. It is not surprising if children avoid insecurity by behaving in as sex-stereotypical a manner as possible. They actively look out for clues about how males and females 'should' behave. Television, with its larger-than-life caricatures of men and women, offers some ready-made ones.

Family members are also very important as same-sex models. Girls are therefore more influenced by their mums, boys by their dads. Children identify and model themselves on the parent of the same sex, especially if the relationship is a good one. From mother or father the girl or boy learns to behave in a 'sex-appropriate' fashion.

Reinforcement

Some types of behaviour are reinforced by reward and punishment. The clearest and most consistent difference in parents' treatment and expectation of children is in relation to aggression. Parents show displeasure towards girls who hit out at other children, and will severely reprimand aggression aimed at parents. But boys are allowed to be aggressive and even encouraged to fight back.

16

If girls are expected to be more obedient and passive, boys seem to be under greater pressure to act like boys. They are more likely to be physically punished and get stronger negative reactions from parents for 'effeminate' behaviour than girls do for 'tomboyish' behaviour. This sex difference in parents' responses could be expected, for there seem to be heavier strictures on boys playing 'effeminate' games, presumably because feminine associations have a lower status in the minds of adults. Thus if a child plays with a gun it may be not only because he sees himself as a boy and 'knows' that boys play with guns, but because in the past he has been consistently rewarded for sex-appropriate behaviour.

Reinforcement techniques can work instead in the reverse direction to liberate children from stereotyped play. If adults become conscious of the disapproval messages they are sending out, and instead positively and openly encourage and reward boys and girls playing with non-stereo-typed toys, children soon learn to follow suit. In trying to counter stereotyped play, women will find it easier to reinforce new behaviour in girls, and male teachers will be more successful in encouraging boys to play so-called girls' games.

It is easy for adults to underestimate the ability of children to adopt the desired or expected behaviour. Children as young as 5 can make remarkably accurate guesses about the sorts of activities parents will approve, and they already know that the rules seem to be different for boys and girls.

Toys and play

Adults often take it as evidence of innate sex difference when a boy voluntarily chooses to play with a car, or a little girl likes putting her dolly to bed. But children positively prefer familiar objects. In a new situation they will seek out toys which resemble the ones they have at home; we know that these are likely to be stereotyped.

An interesting study of toys bought for children in the pre-Christmas period showed that boys received more expensive toys and that girls were more frequently bought clothes, furniture or jewellery instead of play-things. Significantly, the more expensive items such as bicycles and microscopes were sold by salesmen, while the salesladies were responsible for cheaper 'little girl' items like plastic ironing boards and nurses' outfits (*MS Magazine*, 1974)!

Girls, unlike boys, are given tools for imitation housework. This actually helps them to do simple household tasks and is a preparation for the real thing. Even while they are still at school girls are expected to help more in the house, which means they actually have less free time for play and leisure activities than boys.

Toys typically given to boys, such as construction sets, Lego, transport toys, chemistry sets and microscopes, are more likely to contribute to the development of visuo-spatial abilities and pre-scientific interests. Unless girls receive experiences at school to make up for what they may lack from home, they may miss out on some important play activities.

Social learning

However, boys and girls are not blind to 'opposite' sex behaviour. Boys and men learn from observation of mothers, sisters or women on television how to put on lipstick. They just don't use their knowledge. Young women know how to put big cigars in their mouths and behave like city tycoons, but it is not often socially permissible to do so. That is why the same boy may refuse indignantly to sew a doll's dress, yet be perfectly happy sewing the hem of a tent at scout camp (Mischel, 1967).

This may extend to school work. D.J. Hargreaves found that 10-year-olds could get different scores on parts of a test according to whether they were 'being themselves', or 'pretending' to be a boy/girl. They had a striking ability to produce the appropriate sex-typed response for either sex (Hargreaves, 1977). Later on, girls will be more willing to admit to finding mathematics difficult - an accepted 'feminine' trait.

Children are strongly motivated to behave 'appropriately', i.e. according to sex role. Their knowledge about what is appropriate develops and becomes refined, as does their knowledge of world geography or arithmetic, in a gradual series of stages. At the age of 5 children know that women are supposed to 'like to hug and kiss a lot' and be gentle, that men 'get into fights' and 'make most of the rules'. At 8 years of age they have learned, in addition, that women are emotional, soft-hearted and depend on someone else to make the rules, while males are messy, use bad words and hurt other people. At 11 they can report on the expectation that women talk a lot and are always changing their minds but men are more sure of themselves. Learning of stereotypes is not complete even at 11, as children of that age do not yet know that women are said to be flirtatious and men to be logical (Best *et al.*, 1977).

There have been several studies in which adults observing a neutrally-dressed baby decided it had different characteristics, depending on whether they believed it was a girl or a boy. Exactly the same actions would be described as 'timid' if the baby was thought to be female, and 'angry' if it was believed to be a little boy.

Sex-stereotyped expectations may be so deeply ingrained that we are genuinely unaware of them. But we can see the reflection of these stereotypes in very young children's exaggerated notions of masculinity and femininity. Even 3-year-old children have been found to stereotype young babies by sex, seeing the 'girl' as little, slow, weak and dumb, the 'boy' as big, fast, strong and smart (Haugh *et al.*, 1980).

One implication may be that 'social studies' or project work on sex roles in society, often considered suitable study for adolescents, would be just as relevant in the infant and junior years. By teaching about social change we can prepare children to be more adaptable in a world where what is expected of men and women between one generation and the next can be very different. (See number 16 in the list of twenty-five intervention strategies, page 68.)

References

Best, D.L., Williams, J.E. *et al.*, 1977, 'Development of sex-trait stereotypes among young children in the United States, England, and Ireland', *Child Development*, December, vol. 48, no. 4, pp. 1375-1385.

Hargreaves, D.J., 1977, 'Sex roles in divergent thinking', *British Journal of Educational Psychology*, vol. 47, pp. 25-32.

Hartley, D., 1978, 'Teachers' definition of boys and girls: some consequences', *Research in Education*, no. 20.

Haugh, S.S., Hoffman, C.D., and Cowen, G., 1980, 'The eye of the very young beholder: sex typing of infants by young children', *Child Development*, vol. 51, pp. 598-600.

Mischel, W., 1967, 'A social learning view of sex differences in behaviour', in E.E. Maccoby (ed.), *The Development of Sex Differences*, Tavistock.

MS Magazine, 1974, 'A report on children's toys', reprinted in J. Stacey, S. Bereaud and J. Daniels (eds.), *And Jill Came Tumbling After: Sexism in American Education*, Dell, New York.

3. SEX DIFFERENCES IN ABILITY

Children arrive at school with a well-developed sense of how boys and girls 'ought' to behave. At present, most schools are likely to reinforce rather than challenge the social stereotypes learned at home. But experienced teachers will be aware of another difference more directly significant to children's educational performance. Behaviour may be largely socially learned, but what about sex differences in ability?

In the early years girls appear to mature more quickly than boys, and are in a state of 'school readiness' about six months earlier than their brothers. This shows up particularly in their command of oral language and their visual-motor coordination. There is debate about whether girls are more advanced because of some innate sex difference in 'biological clocks' or whether the relationship is rather with the differential treatment of girls and boys by parents. Existing evidence is consistent with both hypotheses and it is likely that certain biological predispositions are exaggerated and reinforced by parental treatment. If parents tend to allow more physical aggression from boys and to reason verbally with girls, this could affect the activity level and the verbal skills of both sexes.

Whatever the causes, the difference in favour of girls on school entry is well-established. Demands made on boys at this age may be more than they can comfortably and effectively work with (Weiner, 1978).

Spatial ability

Spatial, or visuo-spatial, ability is the only aspect of intellectual performance in which boys often seem to do better than girls. It is generally taken to mean the ability mentally to rotate two- or three-dimensional objects in space. Figure 2 is an example from a spatial test for children.

There are also consistent sex differences in the related capacity to 'break set' or restructure a problem in a new way; this capacity is usually called 'field independence' and males perform better on such tests. For instance, the embedded figures test evaluates the ability to respond to one aspect of a stimulus situation without being greatly influenced by the background or 'field'. Figure 3 is an example from an embedded figures test.

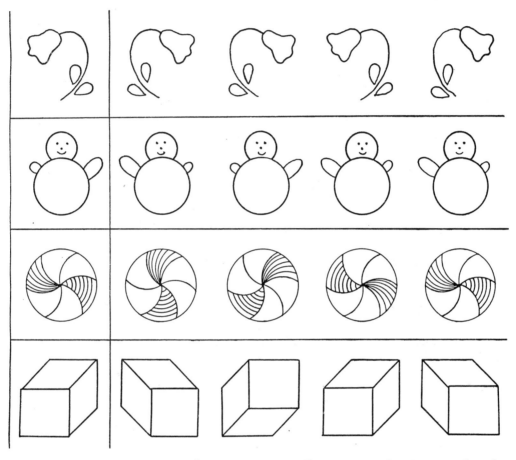

'Put your finger on the one in the box, and find the one in the row that is just like the one in the box. Now take your pencil and mark it.'

Figure 2 Spatial test for children

Reproduced by special permission of the publisher, Consulting Psychologists Press (Palo Alto, CA), from the *Developmental Test of Visual Perception* by Marianne Frostig, copyright 1963.

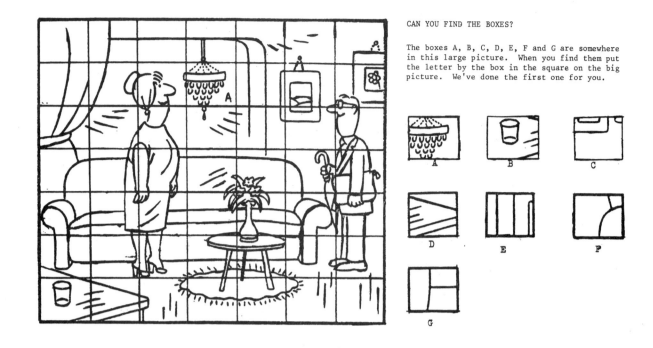

CAN YOU FIND THE BOXES?

The boxes A, B, C, D, E, F and G are somewhere in this large picture. When you find them put the letter by the box in the square on the big picture. We've done the first one for you.

Figure 3   GIST Spatial Visualization: embedded figures test

Source: Girls into Science and Technology Project, Spatial Visualization Test, GIST, Manchester, 1980.

Visuo-spatial awareness is not directly taught in the way that reading and counting are. This could mean either that it is an innate capacity, or that it is somehow picked up in a variety of activities. Very young boys and girls do not differ on spatial tests, but by the early school years boys on average do better than girls.

Male spatial superiority is the crucial, indeed the only viable, remaining argument in favour of the idea that boys' and girls' intellects are biologically different. What is the state of the biological evidence to date? Two main biological theories have recently been put forward:

Recessive gene theory. The first depends on three 'ifs':

      if there is such a thing as a 'visuo-spatial' gene,
      if it is carried on the X chromosome, and
      if it is a recessive rather than a dominant gene,

then boys would be more likely to inherit it. This is because males inherit only one X chromosome, with all its genetic information, and a Y chromosome which is what makes them male. Girls have their 'genetic programme' spread across their two X chromosomes. When a recessive gene on one X chromosome is paired with a dominant gene on the other, its effect will be cancelled out. This can sometimes happen with females, but never with males because they only have one X chromosome anyway.

22

So if there is a recessive 'visuo-spatial' gene, more boys would be likely to inherit spatial ability.

The existence of such a gene is, of course, purely speculative. One way of testing it is by studying patterns of correlation between parents' and sons' and daughters' spatial ability. But recent experiments, using larger samples than previously, have failed to confirm that any such correlations exist (Gray, 1981).

Some writers have tried to make genetic theory more convincing by arguing that there is a recessive gene activated by male hormones (androgens). The *hormone theory* uses trials carried out on animals, with inconclusive results so far. For example, the male hormone testosterone acts during early development to produce aggression in male rats but the same sort of process does not occur with monkeys. We cannot be sure in any case that hormonal influences on human behaviour are similar to those on rats.

Brain lateralization theory tries neatly to encompass verbal and spatial ability differences. The left hemisphere of the brain is said to coordinate linguistic skills and the right to coordinate spatial skills, and it is argued that the left side of the brain develops earlier in girls, giving them relative linguistic superiority, and a tendency to 'left-side cerebral dominance'. The left side of boys' brains is said to develop later, making the right side of their brains dominant and giving them spatial competence.

There are still considerable problems with each of these theories, and so far the verdict on a biological sex difference in ability has to be considered 'not proven'. For primary teachers, the practical implications are minimal. Findings on sex differences in spatial ability are inconsistent and girls can sometimes do as well as, or even better than, boys on certain items. It has also been shown that practical training can improve children's scores, suggesting spatial ability may be learned rather than innate. It could well be, for instance, that the toys and activities more commonly taken up by boys help to develop their spatial ability.

General intelligence

It is not possible to chart intelligence differences between the sexes, partly because most intelligence tests have been standardized to eliminate certain items on which girls tended to do better. On the first Stanford-Binet intelligence tests, for instance, girls' scores were 2-4 per cent higher than boys' at every age level; items have since been manipulated to bring about equal average scores for males and females. But in IQ tests as given, girls tend to score somewhat higher in pre-school years and boys in secondary school years, while both sexes are level in the junior years.

In the primary school, girls seem to be more 'able' at least on the measures of intellectual ability schools generally use. But in secondary school, the position is almost reversed; boys begin to forge ahead, especially in mathematics and science. Any relationship between ability and achievement seems to be complicated by the factor of sex.

Verbal ability

From the very earliest point at which children's intellectual performance can be evaluated, there is a tendency for girls to have somewhat higher scores on all kinds of achievement tests. Girls learn to speak, to read and to count at earlier ages than boys. Through the years of primary education girls exceed boys in most aspects of verbal performance. Achievement testing of number ability and arithmetical computation during the junior school years shows little sex difference.

Research surveys have shown time and time again that little girls are on average superior to their male counterparts in most aspects of verbal performance, and that throughout the school years girls excel in grammar, spelling and fluency. It is also well established that boys predominate among backward readers. Among those with reading problems the ratio of boys to girls can be as much as 6:1 depending upon age and level. Girls are better readers, on average, and their reading scores are still slightly higher than boys at the age of 11. But by the end of primary school, boys' and girls' *attitudes* to reading are quite distinctive; girls like to read on their own and they enjoy long, thick books, while boys prefer comic books, annuals and shorter books (APU, 1981).

Mathematical ability

There are few differences between boys and girls in mathematical competence at primary level; those that do exist show girls as being slightly ahead of boys.* This is rather surprising, for two reasons - girls are not 'supposed' to be good at maths, and at secondary school they do not do as well as boys.

A current study of children's mathematical learning in infant and primary school points out that girls' early good performance in mathematics is generally explained away as unimportant or insignificant, and thus devalued: 'they're only good at computation' or 'they only follow the rules, they don't have proper mathematical concepts' (Walden and Walkerdine, 1982). Primary teachers may be unimpressed by the demonstrable superiority of their female pupils because they see it as a purely temporary phenomenon. Biological explanations of girls' lesser achievement in mathematics usually hinge upon sex differences in spatial ability. Yet the term 'spatial' has been used to connote a motley collection of skills which may have little to do with mathematics.

One sex difference in relation to mathematics emerges rather clearly: boys are if anything over-confident of their ability, while girls may not realize how well they are actually doing. Significantly more boys than girls think that they are quick to understand a new mathematical idea, that they are usually correct in their work, and that mathematics is one of their better subjects. The issue of confidence in learning may be a key one here. Boys believe and expect they will do well in mathematics.

----

* A teacher who immediately wants to say that this does not fit his/her experience should remember that, as with all cognitive sex-related differences, the magnitude of sex difference may be trivially small. To say it is a 'significant' difference merely means one can find it in any sufficiently large sample, not that it necessarily has powerful implications for teaching.

They are more persistent when working on new or difficult problems, while girls prefer to repeat tasks at which they have previously succeeded.

As far as reading is concerned, exactly the opposite is true. Girls are more persistent when faced with difficult words. The attitude of a learner crucially determines the motive and ability to learn. Girls are keen on reading and, though primary girls like mathematics, they are slightly unsure of their ability in it. It is part of the 'feminine' role to lack confidence in mathematics; it must also be debilitating to one's performance if one expects to fail.

Boys are expected to be active and restless, and they may perceive the 'reader role' as being passive and conforming (Zimet, 1976). Therefore boys like mathematics, in which they are expected by their teachers to do well (at least in the future) and are less fond of reading. As most teachers will have noticed, boys are not as proficient readers as female classmates of the same age.

Reading ability

Nobody has propounded a 'reading gene' theory. Boys' greater difficulties in reading are usually explained by their slower maturation, or by a number of social and school-based factors.

A popular but controversial explanation was offered in the 1960s by an American, Patricia Sexton, who wrote a book called *The Feminized Male* (1970) in which she argued that elementary schools emasculated little boys by their heavily feminine atmosphere and norms, and that in consequence boys did not learn as well as in the more masculine atmosphere of the secondary school. This idea seemed in some way to be borne out by the finding that in Germany, where many elementary teachers are men, there was very little difference between the sexes in reading ability. But a larger study of reading in Canada, USA, England and Nigeria suggests a different explanation (Johnson, 1973/4). In the USA and Canada girls were better readers, while in England and Nigeria boys did better. Johnson thinks that in North America adults see reading as a somewhat effeminate pastime, and the teachers believe girls are better readers. But in Nigeria, since only primary schooling is generally available and it is more highly valued for boys, reading has come to be seen as a 'masculine' activity. Certainly, all the Nigerian teachers believed that boys were better readers. In England, one-third of the teachers thought boys were better, two-thirds that girls were better. Reading ability may be seen as a component of educational success in England, and therefore important for boys.

Some of the contradictions in this area of research may be partly explained by changes in the content of reading tests. In the 1920s, 30s and 40s 'item content' was chiefly drawn from the humanities. More recently practical and scientific items have been added, and these may in fact favour boys, who according to some researchers, compensate for language difficulties by developing enriched vocabularies in their interest areas (Monteith, 1979).

Poor readers are not only more likely to be boys, but also to be maladjusted and anti-social. And whereas reading difficulties in girls tend to be associated with low intelligence, the same is not true for boys.

Primary school differences: developmental or biological?

We can now summarize what is known about sex differences in intellectual ability and educational attainment amongst primary school children.

Girls get off to a headstart in all aspects of achievement; on British school tests including verbal and numerical measures they are superior to boys - markedly so at first, and slightly so by the age of 11. Boys on average are poorer readers, but after the age of 8 they tend to score higher on tests of visuo-spatial ability, most of the time. Performance on mathematical tests is roughly equal up to the age of 11. Consistent sex differences in favour of the male sex do not make their appearance until the secondary school years.

The conventional explanation for this pattern of sex differences in ability is as follows: the differences favouring girls (reading, verbal abilities) are maturational or developmental, and so disappear with age, that is when the boys catch up. The differences favouring boys (maths and visuo-spatial ability) are biologically determined. Boys *must* succeed in mathematics and science, but for girls success in these fields doesn't matter as much. Clearly if this traditional account is accepted it makes sense to try to remedy boys' deficiencies, but is a waste of time to put any efforts into improving girls' performance.

This is probably why we have in the past 'adjusted' both IQ scores and 11+ standards so that boys' apparent attainment is artificially increased. The implicit justification for boosting boys' scores in this way lies in the expectation that they will catch up and eventually overtake girls in later school years. It is also probably why most primary schools provide remedial reading classes, used disproportionately by boys, but offer no specific teaching for spatial ability which could benefit mainly girls.

It is of course possible that the expectation that boys are bound to do better in the end, in so far as it exists in the minds of most adults, including teachers, may itself be a factor contributing to their better achievement. Primary teachers have reported that girls' work was better than boys' in content, maturity, presentation and intellectual level, while believing that boys were more 'truly' intelligent, creative or even brilliant than girls (Clarricoates, 1980).

Secondary school attainment

The outcome of learning processes in the junior years somehow leads to girls' relatively poorer achievement by the end of secondary schooling. This underachievement is easily hidden. Girls actually obtain more O levels on average than boys, so in one sense they seem to be doing quite well (see Figure 4).

As this 'gender spectrum' of school subjects shows, girls collect exam passes over a wider range of subjects. But some of their qualifications don't actually lead anywhere. Boys may have fewer passes, but they are in more useful and marketable subjects, such as physical science, mathematics and technology. This is why, regardless of school-leaving qualifications, boys are more likely to receive further education and training.

26

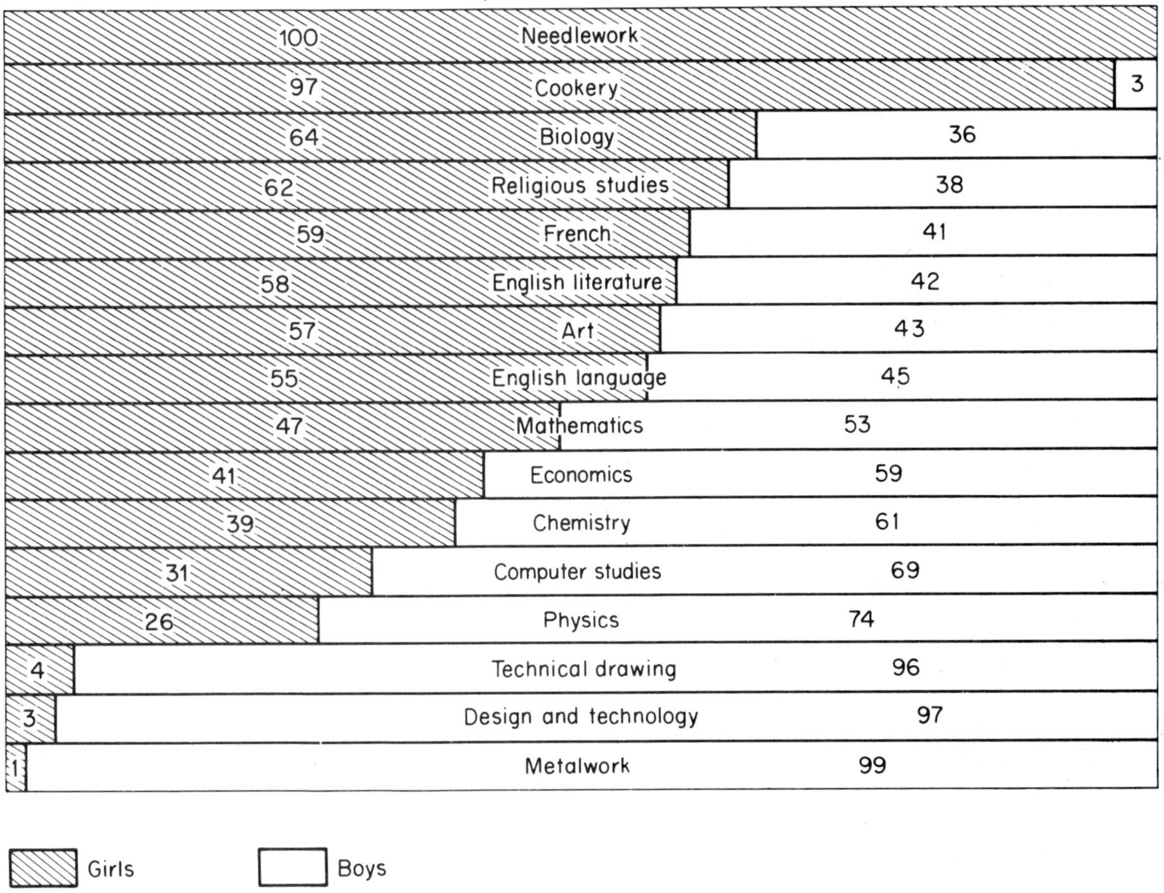

100	Needlework	
97	Cookery	3
64	Biology	36
62	Religious studies	38
59	French	41
58	English literature	42
57	Art	43
55	English language	45
47	Mathematics	53
41	Economics	59
39	Chemistry	61
31	Computer studies	69
26	Physics	74
4	Technical drawing	96
3	Design and technology	97
1	Metalwork	99

▨ Girls   ☐ Boys

Figure 4 Gender spectrum: percentages of girls and boys entering for O levels, England, summer 1981

Source: Compiled by the author from DES and Examination Board figures.

Table 1 Percentage of men and women improving their level of qualifications after leaving school

Level of qualifications achieved at school							
None or sub-GCE		O level		A level		Overall	
Men	Women	Men	Women	Men	Women	Men	Women
25.0	21.8	51.5	29.1	78.1	78.6	36.5	28.6

Source: J.W.B. Douglas and N. Cherry, 'Does sex make any difference?', *Times Educational Supplement*, 9/12/77.

It is clear from Table 1 that the women who leave school with O levels are most deprived of opportunities to increase qualifications, i.e. over half the men who had left school with O levels gained further qualifications later on, compared with less than one-third of the women. For the women who leave school with minimal qualifications, the chances of obtaining training for employment are low in comparison with those of men (see Table 2). And while in the past, girls with A levels were just as likely as their male peers to go on to higher education, the contraction in teacher training has severely cut back on the number of higher education places for women.

Table 2 New entrants to employment: type of work and training (percentages rounded up)

	Men	Women
	%	%
Apprenticeship or learnership for skilled occupation	43	7*
Employment leading to recognized professional qualifications	1	2
Clerical employment	7	40
Other employed with planned training lasting more than 52 weeks	10	6
Other employment with planned training lasting 8-52 weeks	7	12
Other employment with training lasting less than 8 weeks	32	34

* Over 70% in hairdressing

Source: Manpower Services Commission, cited in M.B. Sutherland, 1981, *Sex Bias in Education*, Blackwell, Oxford.

The problem does not seem to be that girls, as a group, are less able than boys. It is rather that the education they choose, or into which they are channelled, is skewed towards a traditional arts and humanities base, so that they lack the technical qualifications which would lead to well-paid and secure trades or professions. They *choose* to avoid science and mathematics partly because of attitudes to those subjects which they have picked up during the primary years. Children as young as 8 have been shown to perceive science as a 'masculine' domain (Harvey and Edwards, 1980). They are *channelled* away from science, mathematics and technology in part because of teacher expectations about the sorts of jobs and futures open to women. The 'choosing' and 'channelling' begin at a very early stage in a child's life.

References

Assessment of Performance Unit, 1980, *Mathematical Development*, Primary Survey Report no. 1, HMSO.

Assessment of Performance Unit, 1981, *Language Performance in Schools*, Primary Survey Report no. 1, HMSO.

Clarricoates, K., 1980, 'The importance of being Ernest ... Emma ... Tom ... Jane: the perception and categorization of gender conformity and gender deviation in primary schools' in R. Deem (ed.), *Schooling for Women's Work*, Routledge & Kegan Paul.

Gray, J.A., 1981, 'A biological basis for the sex differences in achievement in science?' in A. Kelly (ed.), *The Missing Half: Girls and Science Education*, Manchester University Press.

Harvey, T.J. and Edwards, P., 1980, 'Children's expectations and realisations of science', *British Journal of Educational Psychology*, vol. 50, part 1, February, pp. 74-76.

Johnson, D.D., 1973/4, 'Sex differences in reading across cultures', *Reading Research Quarterly*, no. 1, p. 67.

Monteith, M., 1979, 'Boys, girls and language', *English in Education*, summer, vol. 12, pp. 3-6.

Sexton, P., 1970, *The Feminized Male*, Random House.

Walden, R. and Walkerdine, W., 1982, *Girls and Mathematics: The Early Years*, Bedford Way Papers, 8, University of London Institute of Education.

Weiner, G., 1978, 'Education and the Sex Discrimination Act', *Educational Research*, June, vol. 20, no. 3, pp. 163-73.

Zimet, S.G., 1976, 'Reader content and sex differences in achievement', *Reading Teacher*, vol. 29, no. 8, pp. 758-63.

4. THE 'HIDDEN CURRICULUM'

The preceding chapters have shown that sex division is still firmly and subtly entrenched in society at large. The influences of the home and the mass media powerfully affect the child's perceptions of what is appropriate to girls and boys. But it is doubtful whether the home, as some teachers believe, is the sole source of sex-role stereotyping. This chapter gives an account of how the experience of school can reinforce traditional sex-role stereotypes.

The 'hidden curriculum' of sex typing in junior schools

Some of our older primary schools are fronted by two grim doorways whose engraved stone arches bear the legend 'Boys' or 'Girls'. We think of them as relics of a Victorian past. But according to a number of recent writers (Delamont, 1980; Clarricoates, 1978; Guttentag and Bray, 1976; King 1978), the experience of primary school today divides the sexes just as effectively as in an era when they could not even enter the school by the same door. This chapter and the next summarize the small but growing evidence from observational and other studies suggesting that:

1   the experience of school reinforces and exacerbates polarization of
    the sexes; and

2   sex-role stereotyping has profound and differential consequences.

The studies highlight four aspects of school life which are supposed to constitute a 'hidden curriculum' from which children learn and adapt to different expectations and standards for boys and girls. They are: the informal interactions between children in the classroom or outside it; common school practices and procedures which divide or distinguish the sexes, often for no sound educational reason; teachers' expectations; and patterns of teacher-pupil interaction in class.

Peer interactions

Peers are still the most important feature of a child's school experience. Age of school entrance, whether to nursery or infant school, coincides with the child's growing awareness between 3 and 5 years, of gender as a fixed category into which self and others can be sorted. The child responds by valuing his/her own sex and seeking same-sexed toys, games and activities (Kohlberg, 1967). Very little has been written about the significance of gender in early adjustment to school. We know that entering a social peer group is an experience both exhilarating and frightening for the child. Its charm is the prospect of being accepted as one of the group; its danger the possibility of exclusion. Kohlberg's analysis suggests gender is the most obvious and significant differentiating feature in the child's social experience. The more social and intelligent the child, the more enjoyable s/he is likely to feel it is to be counted as one of a group, even such a large group as 'the girls' or 'the boys', and the more eagerly s/he will learn to play a convincing part as 'girl' or 'boy'.

In both sexes, the tendency to conform to conventional sex role behaviour is exaggerated when others are present. In a study set in a playroom, L. Serbin found that children who had played with cross-sex toys (boys with dishes and dolls, girls with trucks and aeroplanes) abandoned them in favour of a 'sex-appropriate' toy when another child entered their playspace (Serbin, 1978).

In the less structured environment of the playground, where older children are present, sexual demarcation may be more crudely reinforced. In an American school,

> There was an intensive struggle for control of a "fort" which the boys had built on the playground. They would not let "outsiders" in. Outsiders included all girls... Girls who tried to gain entry on one day were physically attacked by the boys, knocked to the ground, and had their coats torn off. (L. Sussman reported in Delamont, 1980, p. 41)

There are comparatively few British observational studies of boy/girl interactions in the playground or classroom. Kathy Clarricoates spent some time making observations in a primary school. She describes the daily battle between the sexes away from the eyes of authority:

> the nooks and crannies and sheltered bays of the old urban traditional school often concealed (from supervision purposes) aspects of behaviour which the boys were not keen to have discovered; particularly when they made the girls "run the gauntlet" outside the toilets.

Female solidarity offered some protection:

> The girls succeeded in perfecting an "early warning system" whereby lookouts were posted in order to decrease the activities of the boys laying siege to the building. (Clarricoates, 1979)

In the playground the implied threat of violence can lead to girls voluntarily limiting themselves to a corner or the edges of the available space (Wolpe, 1977, p. 39). In junior schools there are sometimes two playgrounds: one for the boys, the other for 'girls and infants'. The division both implies and enforces more restraint on girls' physical play.

Hostilities have to be carried on in a milder form under a teacher's eye in the classroom. Nursery and infant teachers in Manchester were asked by a local authority working party to observe their class during 'free activity' periods. Almost one-third of the comments spontaneously drew attention to the more 'robust' or 'boisterous' behaviour of the boys:

> It was observed that ... boys tend to play in gangs more than girls and that in their play they seem to adopt a more aggressive role, e.g. three or four boys will make a "raid" on the Wendy House and threaten those playing there. (Infant Teacher, 1981)

> I usually say only one boy at a time in the Wendy House
> (plus three girls), otherwise the boys want to play "wars".
> (Infant Teacher, 1981)

> When boys do choose to play here [in the Wendy House] they
> often want to be robbers or dogs! (Infant Teacher, 1981)

One can visualize what is happening here as the girls, with teacher's implicit support, define the Wendy House as 'their' territory, which boys may enter only under certain conditions. Two further comments:

> The boys tended to play a passive role, allowing themselves
> to be fussed over by the girls. (Infant Teacher, 1981)

> The number of boys and girls playing in the Wendy House is
> pretty even but the girls sometimes object to the boys
> trying to play the "woman's role". (Infant Teacher, 1981)

Sets of observations were recorded for over 100 nursery and infant classes. No monitoring of the observations was undertaken, but analysis of the figures returned by the teachers indicates that children's choices became more sex-typed between nursery and infant classes (see Table 3).

Table 3 Children's choices of play

Activity	Age group 3-5 (Nursery)		Age group 5 and over (Infant)	
	% boys	% girls	% boys	% girls
Wendy House/Home Corner	42	58	34	66
Dolls' house	46	54	22	78
Constructional play	64	36	66	34
Bricks, cars, trains	69	31	73	27
'Feminine' activity:	*Fewer* boys and *more* girls participate in older age group			
'Masculine' activity:	More *boys* but *fewer* girls participate in older age group			

Source: Unpublished survey by local authority working party, Manchester, 1981.

This pattern suggests that we should be very cautious about assuming children are exhibiting merely 'natural' differences of interest. While these may exist, the effect of peer interactions excluding each sex from the other's area may be to exaggerate initial differences. For children so young, whatever their sex, the 'Home Corner' or 'Wendy House' has obvious associations with comfort, security and home. The small boys who played at being 'robbers and dogs' were perhaps unwilling outsiders, learning a rather hard lesson in independence. Little wonder if they should react by defining the world outside 'home' as boys' territory:

Boy 1: Come on - the boat's going to Africa.

Boy 2: Yeah - come on: we're taking the lions home. No, you can't come on the ship.

Girl 1: Why? I'm playing with you - I'm one of the lions.

Boy 1: You don't get girls on ships.

Girl 2: Why not?

Boy 3: You just don't that's all!

(Unpublished draft, Devon Education Department, 1978)

In the school life of one child there may be a thousand such apparently trivial and unrecorded interactions. The child learns, as surely as if s/he had been taught, that certain games, activities and even physical spaces are for girls or boys. That perception is reinforced by some of the common rules and practices of the school.

School practices

School organization segregates the children by sex from the very first day. Boys and girls have separate lavatories, cloakrooms and sometimes playspaces; they line up separately and often sit separately in assembly, at just the point in the day when 'unity' and school ethos are emphasized. The seemingly insignificant practice of listing children by sex on the register can also lead to their being called out of class separately to see the school nurse/psychologist/photographer (Delamont, 1980). These practices confirm and give official sanction to the child's realization that gender is the fundamentally important aspect of one's personality as a pupil, and defines the group to which one belongs.

Few primary schools insist on school uniform but all see children's dress as having disciplinary as well as social significance. Rules about pupils' clothing underpin the orthodoxy and the ethics of the school, and also satisfy a desire on the part of both parents and teachers that the child appear respectable, i.e. middle-class rather than working-class. (Jackson and Marsden, 1966, pp. 47, 125). Boys may have to wear short trousers, girls skirts and dresses. The restrictions have certain specific effects on girls. Nursery teachers compliment girls on their appearance more than boys, and more when they are wearing dresses than trousers (Delamont, 1980, pp. 35-6). Girls, in other words, are praised for merely looking pretty, not for any achievement. Adults often fuss when children dirty their clothes, but more displeasure is expressed when a girls gets her 'nice clean frock' dirtied. Girls' unwillingness to get dirty can inhibit them from participating in various types of educational play, e.g. using climbing frames, playing on the floor, or using messy materials.

On purely practical grounds, good quality dungarees or long trousers for both sexes would be warmer in winter, easier to clean and more suitable for messy, active play. For summer wear, recent medical opinion is strongly supportive of all children uncovering their limbs, and doctors would recommend shorts and short dresses for boys and girls. The point has been well recognized by educational radicals who often relaxed rules about dress as a first step towards 'liberating' the child.

> Every child has the right to wear clothes of such a kind
> that it does not matter a brass farthing if they get messy
> or not. (Neill, 1968, p. 112)

Teachers' expectations

In a large study which followed children from birth it was found that on
arrival at school, children were not yet heavily sex typed. Viewed as
individuals, their needs and impulses were remarkably similar. Parents
had stereotyped expectations of what the baby would be like, depending
on its sex. But their stereotyped expectations were soon replaced by
more individual expectations six months after the birth (Jacklin, 1980).
Once parents have had the opportunity to observe their offspring at
close quarters, they acknowledge and accept unconventional behaviour:
that Janet likes to climb trees rather than play house, for instance,
or that Tommy cannot be parted from his dolly without floods of tears.
Parents continue to have stereotyped assumptions about boys and girls
in general, but are prepared to make exceptions for individual children's
preferences, even if these are unusual.

To the reception teacher, Janet, Mary and Tommy are strangers, two or
three out of a group of twenty-five or so. Where children are not known
individually, the tendency is to group them or categorize them on the
basis of superficial differences. We know that infant teachers, by using
clues of appearance and speech, tend to overrate the ability of middle-
class children and underrate working-class children (Goodacre, 1967).
Dress is an immediate clue to gender, and in much the same way girls are
stereotyped ahead of time as passive, boys as aggressive. There are
several studies in which groups of adults have been shown the same child,
presented to one group as a boy, wearing 'boy's' clothes, and to the
other as a girl. For instance, students were shown a videotape of a baby
being presented with various toys, and if they thought it was a boy
described 'his' reaction to a jack-in-the-box as 'anger'. Other students
were shown the same tape of the same baby but, believing it to be a girl,
described 'her' reaction as 'fear' (Condry and Condry, 1976). In a
similar experiment, a film of a baby dressed in yellow was shown to
groups of child-care professionals. If they thought the baby was a boy,
they described it as angry when it cried; if a girl, as frightened
(Delamont, 1980, p. 23).

Teachers of young children, according to one study, assume
that girls are better behaved, play more often in the Wendy House and
clean up more readily, while boys play with bricks and have greater
physical strength (Chasen, 1975). These teachers also tend to encourage
the very behaviour they believe exists, for instance by complimenting
boys, but not girls, on their strength. Adults generally are more alert
and sensitive to children's behaviour when it fits in with sex role
expectations.

Observations in a nursery school showed that if a boy hit another child
or broke something, teachers were three times more likely to notice than
if a girl had done the same thing. Their response was also different.
When a boy had been 'naughty' in this way, he usually got a loud, public
scolding. Everyone in the room would be made aware of the boy's naughtiness. But little girls who were aggressive or naughty in the same way
tended to receive a brief, soft rebuke which others could not hear.

We have comparatively little information about how children react to differential treatment of this kind. Commonsense observation suggests that while a few little boys may burst into tears, the majority acquire a sort of bravado and become hardened. After a scolding before the whole class boys may swank around a bit, not at all averse to the gratifying public attention.

Because girls are reprimanded quietly, if at all, they may deduce that naughty behaviour fails to get them attention and so attempt to get it by being 'good'. Girls in primary school are significantly more anxious to please the teacher than boys. This is an example of one way in which teachers' expectations, by reinforcing sex stereotypical behaviour, may become self-fulfilling. Children may be learning to respond in the way that seems to be expected of them. It would, of course, be unfair to suggest that teachers are acting any differently than other adults in their treatment of children. But if differential treatment tends to bring about educational consequences which are disadvantageous to each sex in different ways, there is legitimate cause for teachers to be concerned.

Lucy, aged 8

Lucy's hand shoots up like a piston, as it has done and is to do constantly throughout the day, and she whispers urgently and insistently, "Miss, Miss."
(Mills, 1980, p. 115)

Lucy is as alert and keen now as at the beginning of the day. Since 9.00 a.m. she has constantly been picking up the smallest detail and, despite being occupied in a variety of tasks, has heard virtually every word her teacher has spoken. (Mills, 1980, p. 126)

The fact that Lucy's answers ... are all correct, leads one to wonder yet again if her mind is being challenged. (Mills, 1980, p. 129)

Mike, aged 5

He has finished sentences begun by Mrs Hilton; interjected comments; asked questions; answered many, both right and wrong; made suggestions ...
(Mills, 1980, p. 12)

...he told me of a fight .. in which he and Billy and Eddie were matched against "the big boys ... the very big boys" ... Such information was obviously of much greater significance than anything that had happened in the classroom...
(Mills, 1980, p. 23)

...he could on so many occasions have been squashed by his teacher ... Instead, his energies are skilfully channelled and put to good use with an art which conceals the art.
(Mills, 1980, p. 12)

The juxtaposition here of comments about a boy and a girl suggest some comparisons between the way two able children may respond and be treated at school. The observer wrote detailed comments on a number of children, and was not especially looking at differences between girls and boys in the classroom. But his notes highlight some significant sex differences in experience of the primary school. Both children are able, but Lucy is more conformist and 'better behaved' than Mike. He interrupts the teacher and even makes suggestions; far from 'squashing' him, the teacher takes care to control him without obviously doing so. Lucy, in contrast binds herself by the rule that you must put up your hand and say 'Miss' before you make any comment. She pays attention to the teacher as much as to the task. Her attention is all concentrated on what is going

on in class - the 'official' lesson. Mike, on the other hand, has a
second focus of reference - his mates and the 'big boys' outside the
classroom. He seems altogether a more independent being than Lucy,
perhaps precisely because the teacher is only one referent point in
the wider world. Lucy by comparison seems confined and restricted to
the microcosm of the classroom.

Teacher-pupil interactions

The disadvantages to boys

Girls are readier to obey the teacher's authority, and more inclined
to conform to school norms. Their achievement in primary school is in
general better than boys' (see Chapter 3). Girls like school better
than boys do, and although this may be because they are more amenable
to discipline and order, it could also be due to the fact that at
primary level they make faster progress, attain a higher level of
achievement and therefore greater satisfaction than boys.

A number of writers have drawn attention to these features of sex
differentiation in primary education and, particularly in the 1960s,
there was a good deal of popularization of the idea that boys suffer
from the unduly 'feminine' atmosphere of junior schools. Patricia
Sexton, for instance (Sexton, 1970) argued that society as a whole
limits women to positions of less power than men but in elementary
schools women teachers are able to exert power over small males.
They do so by requiring them to conform to a 'feminine' standard of
passive, dependent, conforming behaviour.

> Boys and the schools seem locked in a deadly and ancient
> conflict that may eventually inflict mortal wounds on both ...
> The problem is not just that teachers are too often women.
> It is that school is too much a woman's world, governed by
> women's rules and standards. (Sexton, 1970).

The theory that passive and dependent expectations of pupil behaviour
are harmful for boys has received support from a number of sources.
Kagan (1964), in a clever experiment showed that most common classroom
objects - the blackboard, the teacher's desk, books - are perceived by
children as being 'feminine'. Teachers seem to prefer and reinforce
'feminine' qualities in their pupils; nursery teachers were found to
reinforce only 'feminine'-typed behaviours, in both boys and girls (Fagot
and Patterson, 1969); student teachers rated as more positive the
conforming, rigid and the dependent, passive children as opposed to the
flexible, non-conforming and the independent, assertive children
(Feshbach, 1969). However there is no unequivocal evidence that female
teachers discriminate against boys, or that male teachers treat boys
differently. Presumably it is primary teaching as such which demands a
'feminine' response. The conventional socialization of boys, and their
expected future roles make this sort of education seem inappropriate.

Feminists have pointed out that learning to learn in passive,
dependent ways may be counter-productive for girls, too, especially if
they are 'better' at picking up on this part of the hidden curriculum
(Spender and Sarah, 1981). They are learning not to be adventurous,
not to question authority and not to take risks, although these qualities
are the hallmark of creative and challenging thinkers. Indignation about

the way primary education allegedly 'emasculates' or 'feminizes' boys, argue the feminists, should be widened to a more general critique of how children learn to learn.

Recently a different case for discrimination against boys has been presented. In the context of British primary schools, teachers have been shown to perceive girls in a more favourable light (Clift and Sexton, 1978/9), and it is argued that girls are 'favoured' because teachers always refer the boys to the girls' good behaviour and never vice versa (Hartley, 1978). However, Hartley also found that boys received more teacher attention, chiefly because they presented more control problems.

Girls' better achievement in the primary years may even be the partial consequence of their better behaviour and the fact that teachers perceive them more favourably. Teachers overrate girls' and underrate boys' intelligence (Doyle, Hancock and Kifer, 1972) and their reading ability (Palardy, 1969). In one study, teachers gave girls higher grades than boys even where there was no sex differences in standardized achievement scores (McCandless, Roberts and Starnes, 1972). This last study was American and does not seem to be borne out by the well-established superiority of girls on a variety of measures and at ages up to 11 in Britain (see Chapter 3).

If all this evidence is accepted, and if it is eventually confirmed in the British context, there would seem to be a pretty strong case for arguing that primary schools benefit girls and disadvantage boys. We do know that boys enter secondary school with on average considerably more problems with reading than girls. Yet the teaching of reading is an area where, although teacher expectations are different (Palardy, 1969), observers have not been able to find any way in which teachers discriminate against boys or favour girls (Davis and Slobodian, 1967; Lahaderne, 1976).

If boys are really feminized and oppressed in primary school it does not appear to hold them back unduly as a group, once they enter secondary school. The reason may be that the demands secondary schools place on pupils - to be adventurous in their thinking, prepared to try new subjects, to experiment, take risks, and operate more independently - fit in much better with the expected masculine behaviour in our culture. Boys begin to value school achievement more highly in the secondary years, and teachers also prefer and approve of boys over girls (Bernard *et al.*, 1981). Boys' actual achievement increases rapidly; girls', while it does not decline, drops behind the boys' rate of progress (Douglas and Cherry, 1977). Unlike their primary colleagues, both British and American secondary teachers prefer teaching boys (Ricks and Pyke, 1969; Davies and Meighan, 1975). They think boys are more robust, creative and responsive in class. Finally, of course boys and girls leave school with very different qualifications and prospects. Girls' school-leaving attainment is not of a kind to fit most of them for the more secure and well-paid forms of employment.

Despite their apparently favoured position in junior school, girls seem, as some feminist writers have put it, to be 'learning to lose' (Spender and Sarah, 1981). The analysis of how they do so is based on evidence from the unfortunately still extremely limited number of class-room observational studies. The examination of patterns of classroom

interaction has been used to argue that girls learn to take a 'back seat' in the classroom, allowing boys to dominate the arena of public inter-actions.

The disadvantage to girls

There is a growing interest in investigating what actually goes on inside classrooms. Some studies concentrate on the type and frequency of teacher-pupil contact. It is notoriously difficult for someone who is teaching to estimate accurately the proportion of their time spent with various children (Garner and Bing, 1973). The findings of most observa-tional studies tell us that teachers characteristically interact with only some of their class, while other pupils take the role of almost silent observers (apart, that is, from speaking to their neighbours, etc.). This is not because of any conscious discrimination by teachers. It seems to be a matter of the way certain children are perceived and then respond. For instance, most teachers will soon stop asking a child questions if s/he never knows the answer or is too shy to speak (Galton, 1981). And yet teachers will allow a longer time for answering to pupils whom they think are likely to give the correct answer (Rowe, 1974).

Almost all teachers interact most with two types of pupil (Garner and Bing, 1973). For ease of reference I will call these the *high flyers*, considered to be hardworking, intelligent, sociable and independent, and the *lovable baddies*, a group who spend little time on their schoolwork and are seen as naughty, but sociable and amusing. Teachers have high expectations of the high flyers; the 'baddies' have to receive a good deal of attention, if only to keep them in order. We can see why teachers might spend more time with each of these groups. But is there any reason to suppose that both the high flyers and the lovable baddies are predominantly or exclusively male pupils?

High flyers. High flyers are the group of pupils who receive most teacher contact; they are the most favoured of all because the teacher has high expectations of their academic achievement (Brophy and Good, 1970). Boys appear to be more prominent for the teacher in a mixed classroom. In particular, the 'brightest' boys appear to impress teachers more than other pupils.

Teachers are aware that up to the age of 11 girls achieve better:

> If you were to compare their scholastic ability, you'll find girls way ahead of the boys...

> I do find the boys have greater learning difficulties.

These comments were made to a researcher in a British primary school (Clarricoates, 1979). But the same teachers also saw boys as potentially more able:

> On the whole you can generally say that the boys are far more capable of learning ...

> Although girls seem to be good at most things, in the end you find that it's a boy who's going to be your most brilliant pupil.

> Girls haven't got the imagination that most of the lads have got.

Why are teachers more aware of boys and why do they think some boys are brighter? A clue to the first question is given in the account of a

'news' lesson given in a Bristol primary school (French, 1980).
Analysis of the lesson showed that certain boys in the class had
developed 'strategies' which increased their chances of being asked a
question by the teacher, and which ensured that during the lesson, they
would become the focus of attention of the whole class. None of the
girls managed as successfully to engage in conversation with the teacher.
Girls' habit of becoming 'invisible' in the class is starkly featured in
some interviews with secondary teachers in another study, where many
teachers said they found it very difficult to remember the names of one
group of girls, and in fact couldn't really tell them apart (Stanworth,
1981).

Secondly, teachers make rather different assumptions about a pupil's
poor performance, depending on whether it is a boy or a girl. In one
study teachers attributed boys' failures to 'lack of motivation' eight
times more often than they did for the girls. Perhaps because some
girls are perceived as highly motivated, teachers tended not to attribute
their failure to laziness or inattention, but to inadequacy.

One consequence is that boys are less discouraged by failure; they
are told and believe that what they need to do is pay attention or try
harder next time. It is an excuse not made available to girls, and may
lead them in the long term to avoid challenge or risk-taking for fear of
being shown up as 'dim' (Smith, 1980).

Baddies. From what we know of pupil behaviour and teacher response in
the early years of schooling (see above) it is not difficult to guess
that, if only because teachers neither expect nor notice girls' naughtiness to the same degree, the 'baddies' will be boys. Teachers believe
in temperamental sex differences (Chasen, 1975) and so presumably expect
that if any pupils are going to threaten control and discipline, it will
be some of the male ones. An initial 'mind-set' may predispose the
teacher to be on the alert for any non-compliance from boys. Expecting
them to be inattentive, lazy or disruptive, the teacher may feel s/he
has to be constantly on guard for any misbehaviour from boys, ready to
nip it in the bud.

A number of classroom studies have tested out the hypothesis that
boys receive more 'disapproval contacts' from teachers. American
researchers carried out a time-sampling observation in three classes
spread out over a year. All the classes were taught by women, and in
each one boys received significantly more disapproval or blame than the
girls did. However, they also received more praise and approval (Meyer
and Thompson, 1956).

Spaulding (reported in Sears and Feldman, 1974) using twenty-one
classes with thirteen male and eight female teachers, produced similar
findings on disapproval contacts. In addition, boys appeared to receive
more of the teachers' active attention. The teachers approved and
disapproved but also instructed and listened to boys more than girls.
The most frequent cause of teacher disapproval was lack of attention,
for both boys and girls. Otherwise, girls tended to be criticized for
lack of knowledge and skill (in a normal tone of voice) and boys for
breaking rules (in a harsh and angry tone of voice). In general, teachers
speak supportively to girls and make more critical remarks to boys
(Lippitt and Gold, 1959). The pattern is reminiscent of the nursery
(above) where girls received a quiet rebuke and boys a public scolding.

We see that baddies are most often boys, and since the baddies must be
kept under control, teachers are highly aware of them. But why are they
lovable baddies?

Lovable baddies. The saying 'Boys will be boys' (there is no colloquial
equivalent for girls) implies an indulgent attitude on the part of
teachers, and adults in general, towards boys' 'naughtiness'. Similar
behaviour on the part of girls may be seen as unattractive. In response
to projective questions, a group of primary teachers disapproved of and
disliked a girl described as aggressive/assertive (Levitin and Chananie,
1972). The authors of the study explain this by saying that an assertive
or aggressive girl violates both the norm of classroom behaviour and a
teacher's feelings about sex-appropriate behaviour. An aggressive boy
is only breaking school rules, not social stereotype. His 'naughtiness'
is neither shocking nor unexpected. It may even make him more 'lovable'.

R. Nash (1973) working in an Edinburgh primary school describes in
detail a number of boys who were perceived favourably although they
were noisy, careless, restless and independent. One was John, described
by teachers as:

> vivacious, mature, demanding of attention (but able to be left
> alone) of high ability, yet poorly behaved, noisy and a gang
> member.

The teacher likes him and lets him spend a lot of time with her. He's
allowed to stay at her desk for several minutes, drawing a camel. When
he has finished he immediately says 'What shall I do now Miss?',
confident that she will respond. John's knowledge that the teacher likes
him increases his self-esteem and satisfaction. Another child blocks
John's view of the board and John calls out 'I canna see'. He 'dances'
impatiently while the teacher finds pins to stick up his drawing. This
'poor behaviour' is nevertheless socially acceptable. Less favoured
boys together with the girls received less attention and certainly less
indulgence.

John is a high flyer as well as a lovable baddie; his behaviour is
condoned not only because he is a boy, and sociable and amusing, but
because he is perceived as 'bright'.

Summary

Teachers interact with boys more, and so are more aware of them as
individuals, and therefore as interesting pupils. Boys are more
prominent in the classroom and girls, by a series of processes of
which they and their teachers are largely unconscious, begin to take
a back seat, and in so doing may 'learn to lose'.

Within the peer group, girls and boys divide themselves competitively
along sex lines and exclude one another from sex-typed activities, inside
and outside the classroom. The organization of the primary school and
classroom reinforces rather than challenges such patterns of sex
antagonism. An unintended consequence is the emergence of what might
be termed male dominance in the classroom and in the experience of
school as a whole, despite initial loss of achievement for some boys.

Awareness of the hidden curriculum is the first step in altering some
of these patterns. Chapter 5 examines sex role stereotyping in classroom

resources, and offers suggestions for good practice which can be
implemented by the classroom teacher as well as at school level.

References

Bernard, M. *et al.*, 1981, 'Sex role behavior and gender in teacher-
    student evaluations', *Journal of Educational Psychology*, vol. 73,
    no. 5, pp. 681-96.

Brophy, J.E. and Good, T.L., 1970, 'Teachers' communication of differen-
    tial expectations for children's classroom performance', *Journal of
    Educational Psychology*, vol. 61, no. 5, pp. 365-74.

Chasen, B., 1975, 'Sex role stereotyping and prekindergarten teachers'
    in P.M. Insel and L.F. Jacobsen (eds.), *What Do You Expect? An
    Inquiry into Self-Fulfilling Prophecies*, Cummings, Menlo Park, CA.

Clarricoates, K., 1978, 'Dinosaurs in the classroom - a re-examination
    of some aspects of the 'hidden curriculum' in primary schools', *Women's
    Studies International Quarterly*, vol. 1, no. 4, pp. 353-64.

Clarricoates, K., 1979, 'The theft of girls' creativity: the early
    development of girls into recipients rather than creators of culture',
    paper presented at Women's Research and Resources Centre Summer School.

Clift, P. and Sexton, B., 1978/9, '... And all things nice', *Educational
    Research*, vol. 21, no. 3, pp. 194-199.

Condry, J. and Condry, S., 1976, 'Sex differences: a study of the eye
    of the beholder', *Child Development*, September, p. 812.

Davies, L. and Meighan, R., 1975, 'A review of schooling sex-roles',
    Educational Review, June, vol. 27, no. 3, pp. 165-78.

Davis, O.L. and Slobodian, J., 1967, 'Teacher behavior towards boys and
    girls during first grade reading instruction', *American Educational
    Research Journal*, May, pp. 261-9.

Delamont, S., 1980, *Sex Roles and the School*, Contemporary Sociology of
    the School series, Methuen.

Douglas, J.W.B. and Cherry, N., 1977, 'Does sex make any difference?',
    Times Educational Supplement, 9 December.

Doyle, W., Hancock, G. and Kifer, E., 1972, 'Teachers' perceptions: do
    they make a difference?', *Journal of the Association for Study of
    Perceptions*, pp. 21-30.

Fagot, B.I. and Patterson, C.R., 1969, 'An in vivo analysis of reinforcing
    contingencies for sex-role behaviors in the preschool child',
    Developmental Psychology, vol. 1, no. 5, pp. 563-8.

Feshbach, N.D., 1969, 'Student teacher preferences for elementary school
    pupils varying in personality characteristics', *Journal of Educational
    Psychology*, vol. 60, no. 2, pp. 126-32.

French, J., 1980, 'An initial investigation into the strategies used by
    girls and boys when initiating exchanges with the teacher', paper
    presented at BERA annual conference, Cardiff.

Galton, M., 1981, 'Differential treatment of boy and girl pupils during
    science lessons' in A. Kelly (ed.), *The Missing Half: Girls and
    Science Education*, Manchester University Press.

Garner, J. and Bing, M., 1973, 'The elusiveness of Pygmalion and differences
    in teacher-pupil contact', *Interchange*, vol. 4, pp. 34-42.

Goodacre, E.J., 1967, *Teachers and Their Pupils' Home Background*, National Foundation for Educational Research, Slough.

Guttentag, M. and Bray, H., 1976, *Undoing Sex Stereotypes*, McGraw-Hill, New York.

Hartley, D., 1978, 'Teachers' definitions of boys and girls: some consequences', *Research in Education*, no. 20.

Jacklin, C., 1980, 'What girls and boys bring to school with them', talk given at Cambridge conference on sex differentiation and schooling, January.

Jackson, B. and Marsden, D., 1966, *Education and the Working Class*, Penguin.

Kagan, J., 1964, 'The child's sex role classification of school objects', *Child Development*, vol. 35, pp. 1051-6.

King, R., 1978, *All Things Bright and Beautiful?*, Wiley, Chichester.

Kohlberg, L., 1967, 'A cognitive-developmental analysis of children's sex-role concepts and attitudes' in E.E. Maccoby (ed.), *The Development of Sex Differences*, Tavistock.

Lahaderne, H.M., 1976, 'Feminized schools - unpromising myth to explain boys' reading problems', *The Reading Teacher*, May, vol. 29, no. 8.

Levitin, T.E. and Chananie, J.D., 1972, 'Responses of primary school to sex-typed behaviours in male and female children', *Child Development*, vol. 43, pp. 1309-16.

Lippitt, R. and Gold, M., 1959, 'Classroom social structures as a mental health problem', *Journal of Social Issues*, vol. 15, pp. 40-50.

McCandless, B., Roberts, A. and Starnes, T., 1972, 'Teachers' marks, achievement test scores and aptitude relations with respect to social class, race and sex', *Journal of Educational Psychology*, vol. 65, pp. 153-9.

Meyer, W.J. and Thompson, G., 1956, 'Sex differences in the distribution of teacher approval and disapproval among sixth grade children', *Journal of Educational Psychology*, vol. 47, no. 7, pp. 385-96.

Mills, R.W., 1980, *Classroom Observation of Primary School Children*, Unwin Education.

Nash, R., 1973, *Classrooms Observed*, Routledge & Kegan Paul.

Neill, A.S., 1968, *Summerhill*, Penguin.

Palardy, J.M., 1969, 'What teachers believe - what children achieve', *The Elementary School Journal*, May, pp. 370-4.

Ricks, F.A. and Pyke, S.W., 1969, 'Teacher perceptions and attitudes that foster or maintain sex-role differences', *Interchange*, vol. 4, pp. 26-33.

Rowe, M.B., 1974, 'Wait time and rewards as instructional variables, their influence on languages, logic and fate control', *Journal of Research in Science Teaching*, vol. 11, pp. 81-94.

Sears, P. and Feldman, D.H., 1974, 'Teacher interactions with boys and girls', originally published 1966, reprinted in J. Stacey, S. Bereaud and J. Daniels (eds.), *And Jill Came Tumbling After: Sexism in American Education*, Dell, New York.

Serbin, L.A., 1978, 'Teachers, peers, and play preferences: an environmental approach to sex typing in the preschool', in B. Sprung (ed.), *Perspectives on non-Sexist Early Childhood Education*, Teachers College Press.

Sexton, P., 1970, *The Feminized Male*, Random House.

Smith, S., 1980, 'Should they be kept apart?', *Times Educational Supplement*, 18 July.

Spender, D. and Sarah, E. (eds.), 1981, *Learning to Lose*, Women's Press.

Stanworth, M., 1981, *Gender and Schooling: A Study of Sexual Divisions in the Classroom*, Explorations in Feminism No. 7, Women's Research and Resources Centre.

Wolpe, A.-M., 1977, *Some Processes in Sexist Education*, Explorations in Feminism No. 1, Women's Research and Resources Centre.

5. PRACTICAL SUGGESTIONS FOR GOOD PRACTICE

Chapters 1 to 4 have examined the evidence that primary schools, perhaps unintentionally, are still teaching children to adapt to traditional sex-role stereotypes. Very often the school is merely reinforcing a lesson well learned at home, or from the media. If schools are to open up wider opportunities for girls and boys, they must begin to offer an alternative view of the possible future for females and males. Sex stereotyping is a matter of concern to teachers because the expectation of passivity and obedience for females, and aggression and non-cooperation for males, seems to be educationally counterproductive in a number of ways. What can schools and teachers do towards constructive change?

In this chapter some suggestions are made for 'good practice' at classroom level to alter or minimize the worst effects of sex stereotyping. Most of the recommendations require rethinking or greater awareness rather than any large increase in expenditure or resources. Changing attitudes may not be easy, but at least it can be cheap! All the specific good practice ideas mentioned here have actually been tried out in some school, somewhere in Britain. Where further detailed information is available, addresses and sources of information are given. The chapter is divided into three sections:

a. School policy and organization
b. Classroom organization
c. Curriculum work

School policy and organization

Staffing structures

Staff attitudes are fundamental to any attempt to counter sex stereotypes in the primary school. What may be less obvious is that power relationships between staff are important too.

In a primary school where both the head and deputy head are men, it may seem to an observer as if they are the real holders of power in the school. Children are aware, even if unconsciously, of structures in which men have authority and women are subordinates. They need the visible evidence of women holding posts of responsibility, if they are to learn that females can be competent and authoritative too.

Even when there are women in formal positions of authority there may be an unspoken hierarchy because of the fact that men always discipline unruly bigger boys, or because the so-called infant head has much less real power than the title suggests. Hidden hierarchies are well understood by participants in the school structure, but until they are openly discussed little can be done to alter them.

Men teachers of infants

There are few schools with men teachers at infant level. This is probably because infant teaching has traditionally been seen as women's work. Ronald King (1978) in his book about infant school, points up the parallel between being an infant teacher and being a mother: 'They cooked, sewed, tidied and even swept the floor. The image was completed by their putting on an apron to do these chores' (p. 72). But one of the teachers is a man, who shares the outlook of his colleagues in the infant department. King concludes that infant teaching is a definite profession with its own identifiable outlook. The 'typical infant teacher', unlike staff who teach juniors, believes in:

developmentalism (Piaget, etc.)

individualism

play as learning

and 'childhood innocence'.

Moreover, the infant teachers express considerable satisfaction with their job:

They felt they were concerned with the most critical stage of education ... Their efforts had visible outcomes: children who could not read or count at the beginning of the year could do so at the end. (King, 1978, pp. 72-3)

Children can benefit from the presence in the infant classroom of males showing they are capable of kindness and gentleness, and of carrying out the thousand small childcare chores which are part of an infant teacher's life.

There is no reason why these aspects of the profession should not equally attract men. Initial training institutions can encourage boys to enter infant teaching. Appointment boards could consider infant teaching experience as a necessary prerequisite for junior headships and deputy headships. Conversely, infant teachers who wish to move into junior school teaching for career reasons should be aided and encouraged to do so.

De-stereotyping the school environment

In most primary schools the main playground space is dominated by boys kicking balls or running about; sometimes the school even prescribes sex division by offering separate playgrounds for 'boys' and 'girls and infants'. The unintended effect is to limit girls' opportunities for large-scale physical exertion and exploration. Schools might:

provide an adventure playground-type area, to be booked by particular groups or classes at different times to ensure that girls as well as boys can use the space;

provide a quiet play area with flowers and plants, grassed over and with small seats;

assign older boys as well as girls to look after younger children;

introduce mixed sports;

teach self-defence to both boys and girls;

train girls to lift and carry, boys to tidy up and help smaller children.

The tendency for girls and boys to separate off spontaneously is reinforced by some of the things schools and teachers assume. Just because professional football is all-male, we do not have to assume that girls of primary age cannot play it. Indeed young girls are often larger and stronger than their male contemporaries. If both sexes are encouraged to play football, netball and cricket, outdoor games are less likely to be confined to one sex. If teachers take care never, even for the slightest convenience, to divide children into girls and boys for any activity, integration of the sexes may occur naturally more often.

When teachers indicate they approve of cross-sex play, girls and boys begin to play with each others' toys (Serbin, 1978). Positively encourage children to venture into games and toys traditionally associated with the opposite sex.

School rules

Some school rules may reinforce sex roles. Staff and parent-teacher association discussions could reconsider the following kinds of rules:

Boys may not use the cloakroom.

Girls cannot wear trousers to school.

Girls but not boys can stay inside when it rains.

Are they fair? Are they necessary? What effect do they have on children's perceptions of appropriate behaviour for boys and girls?

Informal norms are as significant as official rules; indeed children often take common practice to be strict rulings.

Are *both* sexes asked to take messages round the school, or is it nearly always girls?

Are only boys asked to heave milk crates about?

Do children poke fun at boys who cry?

Are girls expected to be more 'mature' or 'ladylike'?

Working with parents

Any change in what is traditionally expected of schools works better if parents understand the reasons behind the change. If staff discussions have led to the conclusion that girls and boys need tough, wearable clothes for work and play in infant and junior years, parents can appreciate the same point if it is openly discussed and explained to them. It is difficult to encourage some girls to become more physically active because they are sent to school in polished patent shoes and flimsy dresses. If the teachers are suggesting the change in dress for sound educational reasons, parents may listen willingly; working mothers and fathers may even be relieved to send children in more practical, easy-care clothes.

Parents are increasingly aware of the importance of science and technology in children's education. A course or evening talk for parents explaining and illustrating a programme for teaching science and technology through everyday living could stimulate them to back up your efforts at home.

Parents may also be interested in the theory that boys are poorer readers partly because boys see the 'reader role' as passive or sissy. Do fathers read at home, and read to their children?

Promotion and staff development

Seventy-seven per cent of primary teachers are women, yet most of the available scale posts go to men. Frequently, women themselves are blamed for this state of affairs. Women staff are supposed to be unwilling to apply for promoted posts. However, older women often meet with discrimination when applying (NUT/EOC, 1980) and younger women may be asked questions about their personal plans which would not be put to husbands or fathers. Partly for these reasons, but partly also because of lack of confidence, women teachers may not seek promotion and responsibility as eagerly as men do.

The average break from employment taken by women teachers is now only up to eight years (NUT/EOC, 1980). Younger women teachers should plan their careers on the assumption that they may well have at least 20 to 25 years in the profession, after the break to have children.

> I never cease to be amazed that women are penalised for having children but men are promoted because they have a family to support. (NUT/EOC, 1980)

LEA advisers, headteachers and deputy heads, and infant heads can positively advise and encourage women staff to apply for promoted posts. Without such encouragement, they are less likely than men to realize their full potential.

In-service training

Some staff - and this may particularly apply to women - lack confidence in areas such as science and mathematics. They often feel poorly qualified in these subjects. Where this lack of confidence exists, many suggestions for good practice can be effectively carried out only if teachers have time and space for planning and consideration.

Positive staff development will aim not only at raising the aspirations of women teachers (see above) but also at ensuring that all teachers are fully confident in mathematics, have had recent and appropriate in-service training in infant and primary science and are aware of new resources and materials as they are published and provided. In particular, heads and LEAs should ensure that women are represented on courses about microprocessors in education *in proportion to their numbers*. Anxiety about mathematics and technology often extends to computers, and some women may need special encouragement and demystification about computers.

Classroom organization

The chief argument for coeducation is that it is more natural and lifelike for girls and boys to work together. However they may have to be taught how to do so constructively.

Getting girls and boys to work together

In most classrooms, boys and girls usually sit apart. This inevitably reinforces and exaggerates sex differences and sex-role stereotyping. What can the classroom teacher do about it?

POTOS

Kevin Karkan, a young teacher who took part in an American school programme to counter sex-role stereotypes (Guttentag and Bray, 1976), decided that even at 9-year-old level, the problem is a reflection of adult interactions. A man and woman simply talking to each other can suggest to others that a sexual attraction exists, even where there is none. Karkan's pupils said they wouldn't go near a *POTOS* (Person Of The Opposite Sex) because 'People will think you're in love with the person', said the girls; because 'If you touch a girl you get cooties or "girl touch"' (a mysterious quality which can only be removed by saying 'no girls'), said the boys. The children discussed these ideas openly and came to the conclusion that of course these notions were untrue. Karkan told them some of his own boyhood experiences and how being seen to cry was made much worse by the unwritten rule that boys aren't supposed to cry. This helped the children to see the negative effects of sex stereotyping.

He asked his class for ideas to help reduce the separation between the sexes. One boy suggested inviting girls to play football, and the children also attempted lining up together. But Karkan found he had to continue having short discussions about *POTOS* and sex roles over several days before any real changes in children's behaviour occurred.

If you have seated the children in broad ability bands, it may turn out that one or more groups is single sex. Children tend to make friends with peers of similar ability as well as the same sex. Seating girls and boys at the same table whenever possible may improve the boys' attainment as well as increasing the number of girl-boy friendships.

Channelling aggression

You have a problem: Certain small boys are always thumping or kicking other children. How can you change this behaviour without drawing too much attention to it?

a Decide what you think about aggression and physical fights. Are they wholly bad? If you think a certain amount of aggressive expression can be healthy, it must be so for the girls, too. Consider channelling aggression by teaching children how to defend themselves. A secondary school in London has self-defence as part of the curriculum. The head-teacher took the view that girls in particular need to be able to defend themselves against street attacks. If girls as well as boys are trained in self-defence techniques there may be less bullying and harassment of girls and smaller children.

b Try not to over-react to aggressive behaviour on the part of boys. Rebuke them quietly in a corner rather than publicly in front of the class.

c If there is a lot of physical aggression it may be a sign that children
   need to let off steam. Are there sufficient daily opportunities for
   horseplay and robust physical activity? See 'Cooperation to replace
   competition' and 'Integrated sports' below.

Cooperation to replace competition

Many teachers believe that competition is a good motivating force for
learning. Moreover, children often seem to like it. Many studies however,
suggest that girls have greater anxiety about failure (Dweck, 1977). Girls
act cooperatively in single-sex groups; in mixed groups they compete only
when the situation requires it. Boys are generally always competitive,
whatever the context.

   The implication is that boys, not girls, need to be specifically taught
modes of cooperation. Reinforcement in the form of praise and attention
for 'helping' and 'friendly' behaviour - showing another child how to do
something, lending your rubber to a neighbour - may encourage more cooperation.

   An alternative motivating technique for both sexes may be to emphasize
improvement on the child's own performance. Each child can have a record
card illustrating, in a form they can understand, their progress and
achievement. Big leaps forward gain rewards.

Helping girls to participate, boys to listen

Researchers are consistently finding that in class discussion with the
teacher, one group of pupils who are mostly boys seem to hog the limelight.
It also seems to be very difficult for teachers to bring girls into public
discussion. Here are some suggestions.

   First, check who is participating most and who least in your class.
It is *not possible* to do this while you are teaching. Ask another member
of staff to observe your class during a discussion on two or three occasions.
Having analysed the results, develop specific strategies to involve the
silent children: e.g. wait longer for an answer to come; enforce the
hands-up rule and don't let any individual break it. Alternatively, evolve
a new system: for instance 'The Red Group' is going to do all the answering
today, Blues and Greens will have their turn this afternoon or on Tuesday
or Wednesday.

   A research study into pupil strategies for gaining teacher's
   attention showed that boys frequently broke the "hands-up"
   rule, calling out and interrupting, while girls tended to
   make asides to their near neighbours. (French, 1980)

When you feel you are familiar with the new technique(s) ask your colleague
to come in again, and see whether her/his observations confirm that you
have succeeded in getting more of the children to participate.* The fact
that boys talk more while girls listen more has been pointed to as part of
a process in which girls 'learn to lose'.

---

* This technique, and an observation schedule to help make an accurate
record of class discussions, are being used in schools on the Girls Into
Science and Technology (GIST) Project. For further information, write to
GIST, Manchester Polytechnic, 9A Didsbury Park, Manchester M2O OLH.

A study of children's games (Lever, 1976) showed that:

    boys play outdoors more than girls
    boys play in larger groups
    boys play competitive games more
    boys play in groups of differing ages.

The conclusion was that boys' games equip them with the social skills needed for 'occupational careers', while girls' play gives them the social skills better suited for 'family careers'.

Girls may benefit from being encouraged to take part in large-scale outdoor games with an element of competition. Boys may benefit from experiences of working cooperatively in small groups.

Broadening children's attitudes

Children have fixed and traditional ideas about sex roles. Many teachers will want to broaden their attitudes, but are not sure how to begin.

An American project which aimed to change the sex-stereotyped attitudes of children has been described in *Undoing Sex Stereotypes* (Guttentag and Bray, 1976). Children's sex-role beliefs and attitudes were surveyed and staff designed non-sexist curriculum materials and classroom methods, suitable for young, middle school and early adolescent children. They found that children could conceive women in non-traditional *occupational* roles, but that stereotyping surfaced in the *socio-emotional* roles. For instance, even if a woman was a good mechanic, she would be unstable and make mistakes. Children think women are not very competent, and they tend to see them always in relation to men. Infants and very young children had difficulty in thinking about people in multiple roles: for example, a woman who is a mother and a doctor at the same time.

You may notice that you have inherited a top junior class which is strongly sex-stereotyped. Children are constantly making competitive or derogatory remarks in the direction of the opposite sex. What can you do to counter their stereotypes?

Let the children carry out their own 'research project' on sex differences. The height, weight and relative physical strength of boys and girls can be measured by the children themselves. Use pushing down on a pair of bathroom scales for comparison of strength.

In contrast to infants, the older junior (10/11 years) is conformist and conventional and firmly believes that social roles reflect social duties. However, this age group is capable of appreciating concepts such as discrimination and prejudice. They can see that average differences between the sexes do not necessarily justify excluding every individual from sex-typed activities.

One aspect of children's stereotyped views about men and women is the way they tend to see women only in the role of wife and mother. When you invite visitors to come in and talk to the children use the occasion to offer experiences which will counter sex-role stereotyping. Some of the younger women police constables have joined the force precisely because they are looking for adventure: invite a WPC to come in and talk about the new jobs women are taking on. Encourage the children to ask female visitors questions about their domestic role. A male artist or nurse could also come in to talk about his work and let children see for themselves that men can be sensitive and nurturant.

Free play

Girls and boys learn at school that certain play activities are for one sex only. Often this is something they learn from one another.

'Free play' *can* result in certain activities being 'accidentally' restricted to the children, usually boys, who *begin* playing with them. It is important to keep a balance between giving children some play choices, and structuring the situation so that children do in fact move round to every play area. Teachers can observe play patterns and keep a checklist. This way you ensure that children are gaining as wide a range of experiences as possible.

Periods of free craft activity are often used by teachers for additional remedial work with slower pupils. It may be noticed that somehow girls always choose to play with the sewing and knitting cards or picture dominoes, while boys get the Lego and construction toys. If boys are pushing in first and grabbing the Lego, or excluding girls in other ways, either structure the choices more carefully or institute single-sex groups.

Boys often work together in groups, teaching one another how to play with Meccano, etc. Make sure all the pieces of complicated construction sets are in the box. Give verbal instructions to girls on how to use the toys.

Helping children get involved in new activities

First of all, are you sure your own classroom methods are not responsible for kids sticking to stereotyped activities? Look at these real-life examples:

> TEACHER: What must you do before you do any cooking?
>
> CHILDREN: Roll up your sleeves and wash your hands.
>
> TEACHER: Right, girls go first.
>
> The boys put on green-striped aprons, the girls flowery ones.
> (King, 1978, p. 43)

> A boy found a snail in the wet sandbox. The teacher took the opportunity for some adventitious teaching. She drew the children's attention to its "horns" and "the little house on its back". When a girl went to touch it, the teacher said "Ug, don't touch it, it's all slimy. One of the boys, pick it up and put it outside." (King, 1978, p. 43)

> Boys close eyes. Girls, creep out, quietly get your coats. Don't let the boys hear you! (King, 1978, p. 52)

Opportunities for spatial exploration and free manipulation of the environment are probably highly significant for the development of certain cognitive abilities. Teachers who are aware of this will see many craft and 'play' activities as important educative experiences.

If you have noticed that girls and boys limit themselves to separate play areas and craft activities you can make special efforts to introduce new toys in a non-stereotyped way. It may be necessary to stress that girls can play with trains or aeroplanes, or that dolls, prams and housework toys are for boys as well as girls. Encourage girls to wear easy-going clothes and not to worry if they get dirty from time to time.

Teachers spend more time with both boys and girls in 'feminine' activities, possibly because they are themselves socialized into 'female' interests (Serbin, 1978). This may mean that few children actually play with 'boys' toys' such as Lego, Meccano or model aeroplanes. Teachers can help to encourage children who are unfamiliar with these activities. When Serbin asked teachers to move to the block area (boys' construction toys) and stay there a while, both sexes responded by following her. Teacher presence and modelling is an extremely powerful factor determining children's play activities.

Constructive and educational outdoor play

See also 'Destereotyping the school environment', above.

Boys have far more opportunities than girls to explore the spaces around them and to engage in 'free manipulation of the environment'. These experiences may be necessary for the development of certain cognitive abilities (Hart, 1978; Saegert and Hart, 1978). As a junior school teacher you may wonder what you can do about the fact that the central yard is always given over to (boys') football. If you are not one yourself, you could try to find any enthusiastic young teacher who will coach groups of girls at football until they have the confidence to join in with the boys. In a Salford school, the Assistant gave mixed football lessons, in school time, to 5- and 6-year-olds. The fact that she was a woman helped break down stereotypes.

Girls may need positive adult encouragement, help and advice, before they will get involved in active outdoor play. Roger Hart describes how girls can be constrained to conform to sex-role norms in their outdoor play by male peers as much as by adults.

> Generally building was organized and engineered by older boys
> while girls and younger boys assisted with water carrying.
> Girls would frequently build subsidiary systems around the
> edges, an activity that disturbed the boys. One day, the
> girls arrived early and began very competent dam building.
> When the boys arrived, they moved in with critical comments
> and much arguing to take over the central dam activity.
> (Hart, 1978)

Few schools offer opportunities for large-scale adventure play and girls are unlikely to find it at home. The school as a whole would need to take the decision that expenditure on such a play area is educationally justified in terms of building confidence as well as indirectly teaching visuo-spatial and large-scale motor skills. Lack of adequate playspace is an endemic problem in the inner city areas, and children's needs seem to have had a low priority with planners.

Curriculum work

Stereotyping in classroom materials

Sex bias in children's books has been extensively studied, at least in the United States. The existence of bias in picture books, reading schemes and children's literature generally is now well established. The bias appears to be of two kinds. First of all, females are under-represented. In all the books written for children, there are more male characters; this is true even when all the characters are talking animals! Girls, women and female animals, if not totally absent, are usually peripheral to the main plot.

The reason for this may be that publishers and writers of children's books are quite consciously writing for boys. They feel sure (possibly because parents/teachers have told them so) that while girls are prepared to read almost anything, including books in which the central character is a boy, boy readers will not accept a book about a girl.

They may be mistaken in this respect. It is true that on the whole boys need to be persuaded to read, while girls enjoy reading. But when boys reject female main characters in stories they may be reacting against passive 'boring' heroines rather than their sex. Boys and girls alike preferred 'Pippi Longstocking' (an unconventional and rather exciting female lead) to male characters in the book (Frasher and Walker, 1972).

The second kind of sex bias lies in the stereotyped way females who do appear are represented. One researcher talks about the 'cult of the apron': out of 58 books studied, 25 had a picture of a woman, and 21 of the 25 women were wearing an apron. They included a mother alligator, a mother rabbit, a mother donkey and a mother cat - all wearing aprons (Nilsen, 1971).

If most of the materials prepared for children are sex-biased, what can the concerned classroom teacher do? All the old sex-stereotyped books cannot just be thrown out, even if that were desirable. They may have many other good qualities, despite being sex-biased. The problem is particularly acute with picture books and reading schemes, for these are materials children spend a great deal of time looking at. In fact most people can probably remember quite clearly the pictures, if not the text, of their first reader. In the world of children's readers, the 'normal' home environment is middle class; daddy goes to work in a car; and mother, dressed in a pinny, stays at home. This relentlessly repeated theme is scarcely 'normal' even in the statistical sense. Twenty-three per cent of heads of household are now women, and two in three work outside the home.

The criticism of sex bias in reading schemes does not just apply to American readers, or to admittedly dated schemes such as *Ladybird*, *Janet and John* or *Happy Venture*. More recent British schemes published in the

1960s and specifically aimed at urban children nevertheless 'endorse a set of sex roles that are even more rigid than our present role division' (Lobban, 1976). Schemes such as *Nipper*, *Ready to Read* and *Breakthrough to Literacy* were likely to have central characters who were male, and the stories rigidly divided the sphere of people's activity into 'masculine' and 'feminine' compartments, with little overlap.*

From reading these books, children may be learning to adapt to sex roles which are already inappropriate for the lives we lead today. It is possible that the effects on boys' beliefs are more profound. They accept rigid sex-role stereotyping to a greater degree than girls do, and in the later school years they may express rather forcibly to female classmates the opinion that science, mathematics or technology are 'not for girls'.

The worry about sex bias in reading schemes therefore is not so much a concern with any direct effects on young readers. It is rather the built-in assumption at an early age in the minds of children of both sexes, that girls will be expected to be, or 'ought' to be, limited to a strictly domestic role in their future lives. In order to counter this, teachers can point out to children that some books are rather old-fashioned and out of date, because nowadays mothers go out to work, daddies bathe babies, men are sometimes nurses, and women can be engineers or members of the police force.

Alerting children to sex, race and class bias in this way can be both reassuring and educational: reassuring, because the 'official' recognition of differences or minorities by the teacher can help all children to appreciate 'differentness'; and educational, because the notion of rapid social change built in at an early stage of children's schooling, can promote adaptable and flexible attitudes.

The problem, then, is that most books and resources used in school underestimate or misrepresent the role of women, and many books are specifically geared to what are considered boys' interests. In order to satisfy themselves about the nature of the available resources, teachers can check books for sex bias. 'A Boy's Book of Conjuring Ideas' or 'Ballet Stories for Girls' are rather obviously sex-biased. They may need to be explained and re-offered to children: 'In the olden days, they thought only girls liked ballet (or gardening) and only boys were interested in magic tricks (or the planets), but nowadays ...'

However, the more subtle kinds of stereotyping are not always so easily categorized. The checklist on p.55 can help in making a quick analysis of books and worksheets in constant use, to check whether they are giving a biased or traditional picture of the real world.

---

* W. Murray, 1964, *Ladybird Key Words Reading Scheme*, Wills & Hepworth M. O'Donnell and R. Munro, 1950, *Janet and John*, Nisbet. F.J. Schonell and I. Sarjeant, 1958, *Happy Venture Reader*, Oliver & Boyd. *Nipper*, 1968, Macmillan. M. Simpson, 1964, *Ready to Read*, Methuen. Breakthrough to Literacy project materials for pupils and teachers are published for the Schools Council by Longman.

1. Count how many men (or male animals) are illustrated in the book.

2. Count how many women (or female animals) are illustrated in the book

3. What are the men or males doing (e.g. running, fighting)?

   _____

   _____

   _____

4. What are the women or females doing?

   _____

   _____

   _____

5. What is the book supposed to be teaching?   _____

6. What is the implied message about sex roles?

   _____

Unfortunately, materials designed and produced by teachers can also reflect male bias. For instance, in an infant classroom, the following wall display illustrated geometric shapes.

Robert Rectangle   Sammy Square   Tommy Triangle   Susie Circle

The example may seem too trivial to mention. Yet in many junior mathematics texts females are notably absent. Mathematics problems are frequently geared to boys' interests, and quite young children see it as a boys' subject. The wall display, with its ratio of 3:1 male:female, but especially with its symbolic reflection of 'masculine' and 'feminine' qualities - hard angular males, soft curvy females - reinforces the 'masculinity' of mathematics.

Teachers will naturally still be concerned that it is often boys who have greater problems with reading. As suggested above, boys may regard as 'sissy' books in which the central character is rather too compliant and well behaved, rather than simply books with heroines. Active, oral reading methods may also help to make the reader-role more attractive. Boys - and girls - will enjoy lessons using tape recorders, face-to-face discussions or playing the 'Auction Game' where the auctioneer describes and then 'knocks down' an article. Programmed and computer-assisted learning methods have been shown to benefit boys' reading development more than girls' (Preston, 1979). In much the same way, spatial games on the computer might be more valuable for female pupils.

Nursery and infant teachers may have noticed that many toys and games seem to be specifically packaged for boys or for girls. If toy packaging is sexist (i.e. suggests that the toy can be played with only by boys or girls) remove the box and place the material in a neutral container. Teachers or children can make their own signs/posters for toys, and label or illustrate them as useful for both sexes.

It is also important to demonstrate new toys, and illustrate their use, in a way that encompasses both girls and boys. If the teacher uses language and examples which indicate they do not think in terms of girls' and boys' toys, then children are more likely to experiment with unfamiliar playthings. Apparently, adults tend to suggest 'nurturant' play when giving a doll or stuffed animal to girls, but allow boys to explore their uses. It is hardly surprising if boys take the things to pieces, or use them in a way that seems to us more creative or inventive.

It seems that girls need special help and encouragement to be exploratory and inventive in their use of toys. Because adults do not expect girls to be creative they normally give them very little encouragement in the right direction. Girls need it just as much as boys do. Roger Hart (1978), for instance, found that parental attitudes restricted environmental exploration and boundaries for girls which especially resulted in their timid use of active toys. The reverse can work for boys. Perhaps it is girls who always play around the dressing-up box, and boys don't seem to get a chance. Dressing-up clothes, hats and accessories for *both* sexes need to be provided. Then boys will feel it is legitimate for them to join in too. Of course girls can dress up as men and vice versa.

Topic work

Just as publishers may be deliberately gearing books to boy readers, teachers may think that chosen topics have to interest boys, otherwise they will 'play up'. If it is thought that girls tend to accept whatever is presented, their needs will not seem so pressing.

Clarricoates (1978) has argued that when they are planning lessons teachers frequently decide that the safest course is to find a topic bound to interest the boys, taking it for granted that girls will go along with what they are asked to do. She observed a primary class being introduced to a project on dinosaurs. 'Oh no', the girls called out, 'not again, we're always doing boys' topics.' The teacher's answer confirmed that this was her strategy: 'Well, perhaps later on in the term we'll do something on "homes and flowers".' For pupils this incident carried a double message: teacher is putting the boys first (again) and dinosaurs are for boys, homes and flowers for girls.

Try never to refer in your speech to 'girls' or 'boys'. It becomes too easy to make odious comparisons between the two groups. Teachers often seem to refer to the girls as if they are *all* well-behaved, or to the boys as if every one of them is itching to be 'naughty'. In effect, teachers who do this show that they expect two different standards from the two sexes; they are merely reinforcing sex distinctions.

All topics should be of interest to both sexes. But it must be recognized that social conditioning will prejudice some children against certain topics perceived as 'belonging' to the opposite sex. Teachers may need to bend the stick the other way. For instance, it can be pointed out that girls should be interested in 'transport' because they will be drivers one day or because they may want to plan holidays travelling abroad when they are older; boys should be interested in how babies grow because they will be fathers one day, and so on.

Even young children have preconceptions about 'men's work' and 'women's work'. A topic about 'the work that people do' could counteract some sex stereotypes as well as broaden children's knowledge about the adult world. A study of kindergarten (infant) children in the USA found that even a series of short lessons caused them to increase the number of jobs they thought women could do (Barclay, 1974). If the information came in the context of other teaching it was even more effective than career inform-ation alone, didactically presented. Children could: report on the jobs of *both* their mothers and fathers (mothers before childbirth if no longer employed) and draw up a chart of their occupations; meet a visitor in an occupation non-traditional for their sex; write about an unusual job for a girl/boy which they might like to do; cut out pictures from magazines to make a collage about 'the work people do'; visit a workplace where they should be shown round by a man/woman, whichever is less conventional for the job. See also 'History/herstory' below.

History/herstory

History is an especially difficult case. Many teachers may feel that all the available children's books seem to be about the history of *man*. Most schools couldn't afford to buy a complete new library of non-sexist books, even if it were available. Writing your own materials in history can be difficult and time-consuming. Some teachers have solved the problem by trying oral history.

Doreen Weston, a London teacher, took an idea from oral history techniques by asking children's grandmothers to come in and talk about their lives during World War II. Their memories showed that women did more than just housework and shopping - they were involved in firewatching duties, for example. The head of this school was a firm advocate of parent participation, and it was a normal part of school life to find a parent hearing children read or helping out in the classroom. However, it was not easy to get women who had worked as manual or factory workers - perhaps they were still going out to work during the school day! The scheme gave the children a more positive view of women's knowledge and abilities, and removed some of the boys' prejudices (Doreen Weston, private communication).

The question can reasonably be asked, did women ever 'make history' anyway? The answer is yes, a few women 'made history' in the conventional sense. It is possible to teach about great Queens, and a few famous women such as Marie Curie, the scientist, or Amy Johnson, the pilot. There are also certain historical topics in which women are the focus - the period of the witch hunts, or the history of the suffragettes. However, more and more historians are becoming interested in a broader definition of social history. This approach is both more suitable for young children and also lends itself to discussion about the role of ordinary women and men in the past. Integrated topic work would look at the history of weaving or brewing, making use of local museums to bring to life the way that people lived in your locality in earlier periods. Like most forms of topic work, this will require a fair degree of research and preparation on the part of the teacher.

Good practice in mathematics

'Mathematics ... was regarded as being slightly esoteric ... the only class-room activity that some teachers confessed to not quite fully understanding themselves' (King, 1978, p. 32). Many primary teachers feel they have never been any great shakes at mathematics and don't much enjoy teaching it. It is important to recognize that mathematics anxiety/avoidance is a very common reaction, especially among women. Teachers could ask to be sent on a short course, preferably one specifically geared to primary teachers or women teachers. People find it difficult to explain their feelings about mathematics because they are personally ashamed of their 'failure'; but it could be argued that it is mathematics or perhaps maths teaching that has failed, and not the other way round.

It seems that the two great causes of mathematics anxiety are pressure of time and the sense of being judged and found wanting. (Buxton, 1981). It is important to convey to children a confident and relaxed feeling about mathematics. Give them time and try to use the analysis of errors as a learning technique. The ability to think mathematically cannot function under the combined pressures of urgency and the threat of disapproval. Observe pupils' 'body language' and facial expression. What do they feel when they are doing mathematics? Are they enjoying it?

Two classroom researchers, Walden and Walkerdine (1982), feel that a teacher often assumes the mistakes children make are derived from his or her faulty teaching. As a result, teachers tend to interact more with children who are confident and independent in maths-learning. Those early experiences may confirm and exaggerate the difficult and unpleasant image of mathematics held by most children.

According to a recent HMI report (DES, 1982), many schools 'were concentrating on computation to such an extent that children lacked opportunities to apply mathematical ideas to everyday life, and sometimes failed to understand the calculations they undertook.' We know that girls are particularly strong on computation, but that at later age levels they seem to have a poorer grasp of mathematical concepts. Perhaps we under-estimate young children's capacity to think mathematically. Specific attempts to improve children's visuo-spatial ability could have a positive feedback to mathematical development. Practical or environmental mathematics, and mathematics incidentally brought in to the solving of practical and mechanical problems, are still too infrequent in the primary curriculum. (See 'Crafts, design and technology in the junior school' below.)

Science

Recently there has been considerable growth in the number of texts and resources available for teaching primary science. However, there is much less available for the nursery or infant teacher who wants to foster scientific attitudes and lay the foundation for later science learning.

The EOC booklet *We Can Do It Now* (Everley, 1981) describes the science programme at Angram Bank Nursery School. These are some of the ideas developed by the teachers:

Colour mixing: Only primary colours were supplied in the nursery; children mixed on their palettes, beginning with dry powder.

Electronics: Children played with a simple circuit using bulbs and batteries. Only the simplest connections were possible because of the children's level of manipulative control.

Another idea for older children is to construct a questionnaire painted on a box, with three possible answers to each question. A simple circuit should be laid so that a light goes on only when an end of wire is connected to the hole beside the correct answer. Young readers should be able to manage answering the questionnaire, if not constructing it.

Study of Minibeasts. Provided the teacher's attitude is one of positive curiosity, children will rapidly get over any tendency to draw away from slugs and snails. They will be interested in collecting and comparing them and creating a habitat for them so they can be studied in the classroom. Small-scale pond study was also tried at Angram Bank, using the museum loan service so that children could look at water snails and learn about the ecology of pond life.

There were also many visits out: to building sites to watch site preparation, the laying of drains and foundations and the different materials used by builders. They went to a local car scrap yard and collected and brought back to school metals, rubbers, plastics and car-parts. A mill was visited as a follow-up to a study of grains and the harvest, and to see water power used as a source of energy.

Science/topic work. Many teachers will feel science is an activity best brought in as appropriate to theme or topic work. A range of studies may arise from practical exploration of the environment. Peter Shaw, in his book on primary science (1972), uses water - which 'seems to have an irresistible attraction for children' - as an example of possible inter-linked sequences of work. (See Figure 5.)

The methods of science. Above all, it is important that children begin to develop a 'scientific attitude' and a familiarity with the methods of science. Primary school already provides children with concrete experiences, and the teacher can use opportunities to get them thinking about cause and effect. If girls don't know how to make something work, give them careful step-by-step instructions. Show that you really do expect them to learn how to do it independently. Serbin (1978) found that boys received more detailed step-by-step instructions in how to solve a problem or do something for themselves: eight times as much instruction was given to boys as to girls!

Craft, design and technology in the junior school

In their 1975 report, the DES deplored the practice of separate crafts for boys and girls in the junior school. They pointed out that girls were given fewer experiences of three-dimensional and constructional activities.

Junior craft work traditionally has a strong art bias. It is seen essentially as a creative subject in which children have a chance to do something with their hands. However, there may be a good case for broadening our view of the subject to include elements of design education and the basic foundation for an understanding of technology. Few primary schools even attempt to teach 'design' or 'technology' as well as 'craft'. But there are one or two sources for ideas.

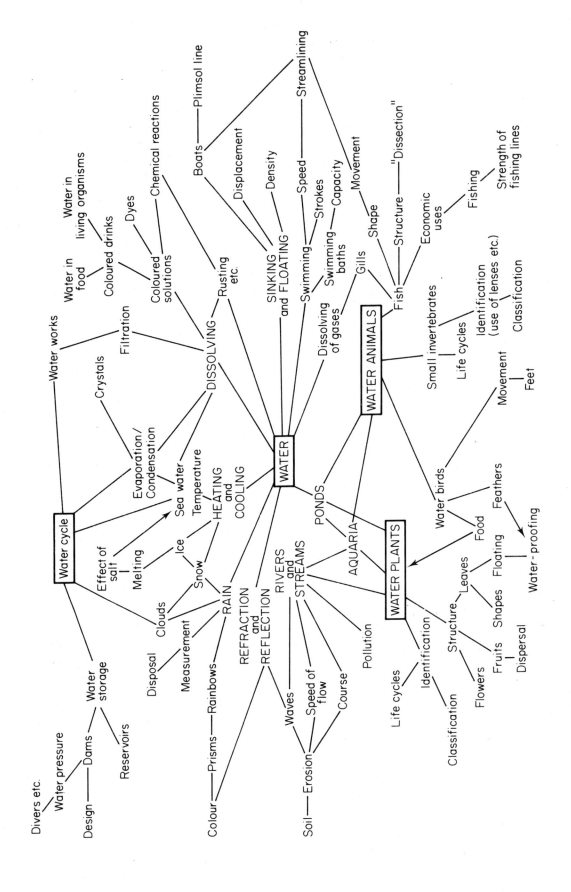

Figure 5 Interlinked sequences of work

Source: P. Shaw, *Science*, Macmillan, 1972. Reproduced by permission.

A pamphlet published by EOC (Everley, 1981) describes a technology project carried out in a primary school in Holsworthy in Devon. They began with a 'workshop' established in a corridor measuring 6' x 10'. The aim was to design and construct devices which could perform some practical function. Girls were as interested as boys, and generally more capable.

If you are unsure how to start, you may be able to set up links with interested teachers of CDT or control technology in the local secondary school. Ron Lewin (1981) has developed some ideas for technology in the primary school. He began by explaining how technology involves people as well as things and that the design process is concerned with solving problems by making something. This is what a child wrote after the first 'technology' lesson (reproduced by permission from Lewin, 1981):

One project was for groups of children to set up a production line for Christmas cards. The winners were those who produced the largest number of attractive cards at the least cost, with Smarties as the local currency!*

Motivation can be a problem. Boys seem to be 'hopeless' at needlework and girls grumble when you ask them to do model-making or play with Lego. Most girls may not play with constructional toys at home, and their reaction against the same toys at school may be a 'familiarity syndrome', i.e. they prefer known play articles.

---

* Full report available from: Fulmer Research Laboratories, Ltd., Stoke Poges, Slough SL2 4QD.

Girls may in the past have been given knitting, sewing, beadwork, etc. on the assumption that they are 'better' at fine motor skills. But boys' fine motor skills thus remained underdeveloped. Both sexes can enjoy 'creative knitting', fabric dyeing, weaving and other crafts which have an aesthetic as well as a craft dimension. If children find traditional hand-sewing difficult, we must ask why exactly are we asking them to learn it in the way we do? Children will be quite prepared to hand-sew for a purpose (to finish off a woven mat, for example); this would mean that they do less hand-sewing and more of other things.

Language work

For whatever reasons, boys and girls approach language work differently. Teachers will want to extend the language skills of both sexes. Moira Monteith describes a programme of seven half-hour lessons on sex-role stereotypes for fourth year juniors. She was particularly concerned with language work, and began with a form-filling exercise which helped the children to think about themselves as individuals before they started to consider what difference it made being a boy/girl.

It was noticeable that although the girls as a group used a greater variety and number of words, the boys had a wider vocabulary, especially in areas in which they were interested. Girls wrote descriptively, but boys seemed to use words which were more precise in their meaning. For instance, boys used words such as: temple, challenged, hideout, veranda, celebrated, protect, battles, captured. One girl used the phrase 'knight things' which was quite appropriate in context, but indicated a reluctance to use the more precise 'armour'.

Children enjoyed their discussions of sex differences and their attitudes may have been broadened by the experience. For instance:

> After Karl had written a few sentences he said that he didn't think girls would be able to wear heavy armour. Craig immediately got out of his seat saying he would find a picture of one and produced from the classroom bookshelves a copy of the Ladybird *Joan of Arc*. (Monteith, 1979)

Liberating drama

When drama is seen as putting on plays, boys always seem to get the main parts and the most flamboyant roles. But drama need not be organized on traditional lines, with a few speaking parts and a large silent audience. Everyone can play if the whole class are involved as inhabitants of a village threatened by a (female?) giant. They can plan ways to defend the village, e.g. the blacksmith will hammer nails through the giant's toes to root her to the ground; the grocer will give everyone pepper pots to blind the giant's eyes with; the church choir will roar and pretend to be an even bigger giant, etc. (See James, 1967, for more ideas.)

Encourage children to take on roles non-traditional for their sex, e.g. the whole class is shipwrecked on an island; children are allocated by the teacher (to avoid sex-typed choices) to the following groups: fire watchers, shelter builders, food gatherers, guards, garment makers, cooks, explorers. The cooks and food gatherers could be almost all boys, the hunters and explorers all girls. When this was tried out with a group of top juniors, the boys were most confident of their ability to hunt and kill a tiger, but it was one of the girls who came up with the solution of digging a pit!

Work in drama can also be used as a way of helping children explore sex-role stereotypes. Role play in pairs or groups can help older juniors explore assumptions about sex difference. The idea of role-play situations, sometimes with built-in problems and surprise elements, has been developed by Kathy Joyce, working with 11- and 12-year-olds. Boys and girls must work together, and an intrinsic part of the drama work is the 'debriefing' or follow-up discussion.

> Situation: The football team needs some new talent. The best footballer in the school is a girl. A playground discussion about selecting the team:
>
> Roles:
> girl, boy, football teacher, headteacher
>
> Role cards:
> *Girl* You love football. You want to be in the team.
> *Boy* You are captain of the team. You want a good
> footballer to join, even if she is a girl.
> *Headteacher* You totally disagree with 'young ladies' playing football.
> *Football teacher* You'd like to have the first mixed football team in the district.*

For further examples see: *Sex Stereotyping Explored Through Drama*, available from Kathy Joyce, Drama Adviser, Teacher's Centre, 137 Barlow Moor Road, West Didsbury, Manchester M20 8PW.

Integrated sport

Everyone is now aware that healthy outdoor exercise is good for children. Primary schools provide for it, but usually separate the sexes at some stage. The traditional arguments for maintaining sex division in school sport have been challenged in a number of ways. It has been pointed out that up to and even beyond the age of 11, girls are as big and strong, if not stronger and taller than, their male classmates. Many girls resent being excluded from the more popular prestige sport of football, and do not accept netball as a substitute. Whether we like it or not, sport has often been seen as an excellent context for the development of the competitive spirit. While values of cooperation also need to be nurtured, some would argue that it would do girls no harm to experience the exhilaration of competing and winning at sport.

Psychologically, the conventional exclusion of females from boisterous sport may have other effects. Most obviously, we know that adult women are less likely to continue with sporting hobbies than men, and do lose opportunities for keeping fit in an enjoyable way. There may also be consequences for the development and acquisition of physical self-confidence and even visuo-spatial ability in females.

---

* This example is not actually contained in Kathy Joyce's booklet but is similar to other exercises designed for 11- and 12-year-olds.

There is at least one secondary school currently offering integrated mixed sports (in Clwyd). There does not seem to be any obvious reason why the physical education curriculum offered to girls and boys in the primary years should not be identical.

References

Barclay, L.K., 1974, 'The emergence of vocational expectation in pre-school children', *Journal of Vocational Behaviour*, vol. 4, no. 1, January, pp. 1-12.

Buxton, L., 1981, *Do You Panic about Maths?*, Heinemann Educational.

Clarricoates, K., 1978, 'Dinosaurs in the classroom - a re-examination of some aspects of the "hidden curriculum" in the primary school', *Women's Studies International Quarterly*, vol. 1, no. 4, pp. 353-64.

Department of Education and Science, 1975, *Curricular Differences for Boys and Girls*, Education Survey 21, HMSO.

Department of Education and Science, 1982, *Education 5 to 9*, HMSO.

Dweck, C.S., 1977, 'Learned helplessness and negative evaluation', *Education*, winter, vol. 19, no. 2, pp. 44-9.

Everley, B., 1981, *We Can Do It Now*, EOC.

Frasher, R. and Walker, A., 1972, 'Sex roles in early reading textbooks', *The Reading Teacher*, 25 May, pp. 741-9.

French, J., 1980, 'An initial investigation into the strategies used by girls and boys when initiating exchanges with the teacher', paper presented at BERA annual conference, Cardiff.

Guttentag, M. and Bray, H., 1976, *Undoing Sex Stereotypes*, McGraw-Hill, New York.

Hart, R., 1978, 'Sex differences in the use of outdoor space' in B. Sprung (ed.), *Perspectives on Non-sexist Early Childhood Education*, Teachers College Press.

James, R., 1967, *Infant Drama*, Nelson.

King, R., 1978, *All Things Bright and Beautiful?*, Wiley, Chichester.

Lever, J., 1976, 'Sex differences in the games children play', *Social Problems*, vol. 23, pp. 478-87.

Lewin, R., 1981, 'Technology alert! - in the primary school', *School Technology*, December, pp. 2-5.

Lobban, G., 1976, 'Sex roles in reading schemes' in The Children's Rights Workshop (ed.) *Sexism in Children's Books*, Papers in Children's Literature No. 2, Writers and Readers Publishing Co-operative.

Monteith, M., 1979, 'Boys, girls and language', *English in Education*, summer, vol. 12, no. 2, pp. 3-6.

Nilsen, A.P., 1971, 'Women in children's literature', *College English*, May, pp. 918-26.

NUT/EOC, 1980, *Promotion and the Woman Teacher*.

Preston, R., 1979, 'Reading achievements of German boys and girls related to sex of teacher', *The Reading Teacher*, February, vol. 32, no. 5, p. 521.

Saegert, S. and Hart, R., 1978, 'The development of environmental competence in girls and boys' in P. Burnett (ed.), *Women and Society*, Chicago Maaroufa Press.

Serbin, L.A., 1978, 'Teachers, peers, and play preferences: an environmental approach to sex typing in the preschool' in B. Sprung (ed.), *Perspectives on Non-sexist Early Childhood Education*, Teachers College Press, 1978.

Shaw, P., 1972, *Science*, British Primary Schools Today series, Macmillan.

Walden, R. and Walkerdine, W., 1982, *Girls and Mathematics: the Early Years*, Bedford Way Papers, 8, University of London Institute of Education.

6. CONCLUSION

This booklet began by pointing to an apparent contradiction: girls do better than boys at primary school, yet in the end they do not seem to benefit in either personal or career terms from that initial advantage.

The processes involved are subtle and long-term. Girls' tendency to seek to please adults is counter-productive for their future as learners. Instead of becoming curious, restless, adventurous pupils, they habitually conform, and avoid risks and challenges. Girls fit only too well into a primary school atmosphere which can sometimes be stultifying in its conventionalism.

The cosy, enclosed world of the primary school is not unlike the Wendy House: it offers pleasant and reassuring experiences to girls rather than stretching or challenging them. These limitations may reflect the more limited qualifications and the more circumscribed outlook of staff who have been recruited to teach in primary schools. Just as the woman who works at home receives less status and respect than the employed person, those responsible for the education of young children have too low a status; here is another example of women's work being undervalued.

Secondary schools are beginning to review the curriculum offered to both sexes, and to recognize that girls have not had genuinely equal chances. A more difficult task confronts primary teachers: they must analyse and overturn a hidden curriculum from which girls have 'learned to lose' even before the 'real' academic challenge begins.

Coeducation in primary schools has become education for and on behalf of the boys. They get more teacher time and attention, and the emphasis on reading skills and good behaviour is designed to compensate for male pupils' needs or deficiencies. Treating children the same seems to mean treating them as if they were all boys. Boys may require to be restrained and controlled, but the same is not true of girls. They could do with specific encouragement to become more independent, assured and intrepid, to take risks, to think and act for themselves. Perhaps while boys are in the classroom, catching up with the intellectual pace set by their female class-mates, the girls should be outside? Sports and venturesome physical activities will possibly help girls develop the healthy self-confidence, courage and independence they later seem to lack.

Children's stereotypes are most rigid when it comes to occupations. The classic example is the small girl who insisted that women could not be doctors, only nurses, even though her own mother was a qualified GP! That small social fact was completely outweighed by the picture of the world she had gained by other means.

The primary school has been slow to adapt to social changes, yet this is where children build up a perception of the social world they will inhabit in the future. Different demands are already being made on men and women

66

today, for which their socialization has ill fitted them. Boys and men are not sufficiently sensitive and aware of others; girls and women need to learn independence and acquire self-respect.

Already we see the need for adults of both sexes who are flexible, competent, independent and self-confident as well as caring and sensitive. By expanding our definition of what it means to be 'masculine' or 'feminine' we can ensure that the preparation for life that children receive in primary school broadens the possibilities and opportunities for both girls and boys.

TWENTY-FIVE INTERVENTION STRATEGIES

A. *Separation of the sexes*

1. Never divide the children into girls and boys for any activity.

2. Train girls to lift and carry, boys to tidy up and help smaller children.

3. Introduce mixed sports.

4. Teach self-defence to both boys and girls.

B. *Books, materials and resources*

5. Alert children to sex bias.

6. Prepare your own non-sexist resources.

7. Where possible buy and use non-sexist materials.

C. *The importance of play activities*

8. Encourage every child to explore *new* roles and *new* activities.

9. Observe play patterns and keep a checklist of children's choices and activities.

10. Introduce new toys in a non-stereotyped way.

11. Encourage girls to wear jeans and easy-going clothes and to get dirty if necessary.

12. Aim to develop children's spatial skills as well as their language and number skills.

D. *Curriculum work*

13. Think in terms of infant science, junior engineering.

14. Encourage mathematical confidence through the solving of practical and mechanical problems.

15. Provide concrete experiences in the classroom and by visits outside.

16. Teach about changing sex roles in theme work, history, drama.

17. Use active oral methods in teaching reading.

18. Teach creative knitting to boys as well as girls.

E. *Classroom interactions*

19. Encourage non-stereotyped social behaviour.

20. Realize that you as the teacher are a role model and focus of attention for the children.

21. Observe classroom interactions with the help of a colleague.

22. Show that you approve of girls and boys playing together.

23. Invite male/female visitors in non-traditional occupations/roles.

24. Channel aggression.

25. Replace competition with cooperation.

RECOMMENDED NON-SEXIST MATERIALS

There is now quite a wide selection of recommended picture books and children's fiction which are not sex-biased or stereotyped. To keep up to date with what is being published, teachers will find the *Children's Book Bulletin* invaluable. Edited by Rosemary Stones and Andrew Mann, the bulletin contains news and reviews of non-sexist children's books. Three issues a year; back copies available. For current subscription details send stamped, self-addressed envelope to:

> Children's Book Bulletin
> 4 Aldebert Terrace
> London SW8 1BH

If most of the books available in your school are sex-biased, at least try to ensure that the school reviews new purchases in the light of racial and sexual stereotyping.

> I've made sure the school purchased and uses a varied reading scheme consisting of non-sexist books. And we always discuss sexism in traditional stories, like Cinderella, and often reverse the roles in such stories. (Sally Shave, primary school Deputy Head, in *Spare Rib*, October 1978, pp. 42-3)

There is a number of voluntary groups and distributors offering books and materials recommended as non-sexist:

October Books offers a review of non-sexist and multi-racial children's books, and a book mail order service. Send stamped, self-addressed envelope (A5) and 60p to:

> October Books
> 4 Onslow Road
> Southampton
>
> tel. Southampton 24489

CISSY (Campaign to Impede Sex Stereotyping in the Young) produces a bibliography, *Non Sexist Picture Books* (60p + 15p postage). Send stamped addressed envelope when writing for information:

> CISSY
> c/o Frances Coton
> 177 Gleneldon Road
> London SW16
>
> tel. 01-677 2411

Spare Rib magazine generally carries reviews of non-sexist children's books and back numbers can be used to build up a useful list. Published monthly, price £6.50 per year. Address: 27 Clerkenwell Close, London EC1R OAT.

It is notoriously difficult to find a reading scheme which will please everyone; many of the recent schemes are excellent in many respects, even though they can be criticized for sex bias. But a supplementary reader offers a way out of the dilemma: *Space Seven* is a new adventure series of four titles for supplementary reading practice, published by the Sheffield

Women and Education Group. Available (price £2.00 + 50p postage) from:

> Jenny Kavanagh
> 29 Porters Road
> Sheffield 10

The Equal Opportunities Commission (EOC) has a set of eight occupational posters for use with primary and secondary school age children. The posters are accompanied by detailed teachers' notes which suggest how they can be used as a basis for simple self-assessment and decision making. The EOC Education Section is keen to hear from teachers who would like to try out different methods of using the posters and who would be willing to report back to the EOC with constructive suggestions. Available (free) from:

> Equal Opportunities Commission
> Overseas House
> Quay Street
> Manchester M3 3HN

A number of theatre-in-education groups deal with sex stereotyping. For example, *Annie Takes Off* is a play aimed at 7-year-olds. It tells the story of Annie, an airline pilot, and aims to challenge assumptions about appropriate interests and careers for girls and boys. Follow-up project work is suggested in the accompanying teacher's pack (£2.50). Details from:

> Spectacle Theatre
> Old Abercerdin Secondary School
> Kenry Street
> Evanstown, Gilfach Goch
> Porth
> Mid Glamorgan CF39 8RS
>
> tel. Tonyrefail 673222

For teachers who wish to begin in the area of sex education, *The Playbook for Kids about Sex* by Joani Blank and Marcia Quackenbush (Sheba Feminist Publishers, 1982, price £2.00 + 50p postage) is available from:

> Sisterwrite Bookshop
> 190 Upper Street
> London N1
>
> tel. 01-226 9782

and

> Gay's the Word
> 66 Marchmont Street
> London WC1N 1AB
>
> tel. 01-278 7654

70